VOICES OF Impact

EMPOWERING STORIES FROM FEMALE
VISIONARIES AND ENTREPRENEURS

Voices of Impact Publishing

Copyright © 2023 Voices of Impact Publishing

Foreword by Melanie Wood

All rights reserved. No part of this publication may be reproduced, stored in a retrieval system, or transmitted in any form or by any means, electronic, mechanical, photocopying, recording or otherwise, without the prior written permission from both the copyright owner and publisher.

Disclaimer

All the information, techniques, skills, and concepts contained within this publication are of the nature of general comment only and are not in any way recommended as individual advice. The intent is to offer a variety of information to provide a wider range of choices now and in the future, recognising that we all have widely diverse circumstances and viewpoints. Should any reader choose to make use of the information contained herein, this is their decision and the author and publishers do not assume any responsibilities whatsoever under any condition or circumstances.

Foreword by Melanie Wood

Stories are the most powerful way to have an impact and create a ripple effect in this world.

I have worked with hundreds of women to gain Clarity and Confidence in sharing their stories on stage, on podcasts, at summits and more.

An opportunity came to me early in 2022 to create this book series to share transformational stories of women making an impact.

Sharing my own story in 2020 in a book series and becoming a best-selling author was a game changer. It was time to give this opportunity to other women to make an impact.

It began as something I'd never set out to do; I wasn't born a speaker, a leader or a business owner. Throughout my life, public speaking was never on my horizon. I would avoid it throughout school and my career for almost thirty years – and I did well to avoid it at all costs!

Not setting out to do what I do today came from one of my biggest challenges back in my late teens and early 20s. I was in an abusive marriage where I lost my confidence, voice, certainty, my way in life, and who I was as a woman to the point that I didn't want to be here.

Then one day, a person came along and gave me hope. She reached out to me on a day I couldn't hide anymore what I was going through, and she asked if I was okay, and for once, I said, "No." I knew I had to be ok with using my voice and what would happen next. Her "Impact" on my life is why I'm here today and why I'm so passionate about sharing stories.

As she shared her own story, it gave me hope and the support I needed to leave that marriage. After meeting her and the years that followed, I knew that I was here for more to help other women overcome challenges and find their voice, confidence, and certainty around who they are.

Life changed for me one day 9 yrs ago; an opportunity to come to Australia for a year, and something within told me it was time for my adventure to begin, which was what I had been waiting for. Before leaving, I was given the book "The Secret" by Rhonda Byrne. Which changed the way I viewed the world at that moment.

Arriving in Australia, I was ready! Ready to take action! Even though I was scared of being in a new country, I built my new life to stay permanently in Australia.

I wanted to help women like you (that amazing lady reading this book!) have a voice, confidence and clarity. To be able to use your authenticity to create and build a skill set for you and your business and your life or represent your organisation through storytelling, public speaking and communication.

I started my business, Speaking Styles, five years ago and have worked with hundreds of women to help them have a voice in this world to share their story, their message, and their value. To be heard and understood in this world and create a ripple effect, as I believe that stories are how we save lives, make a change, heal ourselves, and help heal other people—giving them hope and permission to do the same.

Building my business for the past 5yrs and working with women is because I knew how to use speaking to create an impact and attract clients. Out of my past experience, I understand what it's like to be in my client's shoes to have empathy and authenticity to work and guide them through sharing their stories.

Doing this work didn't come without its challenges; over 2 years ago, I was 3 days out from living in my car when the big C hit; 6 months before that, I was in debt and struggling to have enough money for rent and food.

I knew these challenges and feelings were part of who I was becoming and where I would be of service in this world—being heartfelt and authentic in everything I do. I didn't get here on my own; yes, I've done the work of the people who have worked with me and guided me over the past 5yrs, and without them, this wouldn't be possible.

I know in my heart that sharing stories is how we create change and save the lives of others, heal ourselves and rise up us all as a collective.

By sharing your story, by communicating your message, by communicating your fantastic work, experience, and expertise, no matter what field you are in. Just like the women in this book are sharing.

At the beginning of the year of 2022, I had this burning desire to create a new opportunity for women to share their transformational stories and IMPACT the world on a larger scale and reach more people. Then one day, only a few months ago, that opportunity came knocking, and Voices of Impact was born, and that desire came to light.

In Volume 1 of Voices of Impact 25 women said yes to being published authors, and it has been an absolute pleasure to publish incredible women's transformational stories. Now continuing the journey in our next volume, shining a light on more incredible women sharing stories of hope, permission and transformation.

In Volume 2 of Voices of Impact, you will read 20 Visionary Women from around the world sharing TRANSFORMATIONAL stories, creating change and a ripple effect in this WORLD.

In this third volume of Voices of Impact, you will read the inspiring stories of 24 Entrepreneurial and Visionary Women. Through their personal journeys of transformation, they have all stepped up with a **Powerful Message** to create an Impact in their lives, businesses and the lives of others.

Change is within each of us, waiting to be heard and understood.

Ladies, it's your time to step up, step out and lead the change!

The world needs to hear your story!

IMPACT starts with you. Are you with me?

Melanie Wood
Founder, Speaker, Author, Publisher
Voices of Impact Publishing

***

Would you love to have your voice heard to share your story?

Reach out x

melanie@speakingstyles.com.au

Contents

Nikki Butler 1
Taku Cooper 15
Natalie Curtis 29
Maree Delaney 43
Arwen Dyer 55
Lisa Goodhand 69
Mary Gouganovski 85
Nicole Grelecki 99
Alana Mills 113
Kitty O'Brien 127
Justine Oldfield 141
Dr Angie Papas-Ginis 155
Lorette Parrillo 169
Emily Pettigrew 181
Sharyn Powlesland 197
Alyson Richelle Ray 211
Liz Rotherham 227
Danielle Simpson 241
Debbie Smart 255
Megan Smith 269
Cat Spratt 281

Rene Thompson 297
Billie Jo Watt 311
Donna-Lee Wynen.. 325

Nikki Butler

'Inspiring change, transforming lives'

"Today is the day to dream, to embrace your purpose, to love, to be kind, to stand in your truth, to live your full potential, today is always the day"

I was 21 years old when I made the decision to transform my life. It has been a journey across all kinds of emotional and experiential terrains, but it was a decision that changed everything. We all know the saying, 'just one step at a time,' prior to that is the moment where polarity and the opportunity to create our future exists. My fear, unconscious blocks and embodied trauma sought to freeze that moment, avoiding the decision and wishing my life was somewhere else. Then I found the magic, that wishing things were different, that was the moment where potential to transform my life existed. When I listened to my heart's wish, that 'one step at a time' created a whole new reality.

I became my own evidence of the transformational power that exists within us. If you were to add up the score of my Adverse Childhood Experiences, it would tell you my life trajectory was bleak, but that score has become invalid. As a young adult, I sensed that the universe held me and my life had purpose and meaning, far beyond my physical and emotional experience on this earth. I paved a whole new way of thinking, living and being and had this inner knowing that my adversity would become my strength. The beautiful thing is, if my life path can change, the opportunity for change also exists for others.

Let me take you back, prior to that life changing moment…

My deep sense of lacking value in the world was shaped from an early age. I was given into the care of strangers at eighteen months old, with my baby brother. They only wanted a baby, but we were a package deal. These strangers carried my broken and insecure attachment with disinterest and could not provide what I needed most - love, belonging and emotional safety. My carer was emotionally unstable, and family have told me I showed symptoms of fear. Although the experience was only for a brief time before we were back with family, it was a formula for shaping my internal beliefs that the world was unsafe, and I was unworthy of love. Trauma became imprinted within my unconscious mind, impacting my adolescent years.

Throughout my childhood, years of insecurity took hold, with our family experiencing the raw reality of heroin addiction. This brought with it poverty, lack of food, transience across two countries, multiple school changes and unpredictability. It meant not having the connection and belonging I desperately longed for. Each new home was an opportunity for a fresh start and renewed hope, but it only added to the emptiness within me. Our family's search for a new life was counterproductive, as the poverty and insecurities took on a life of their own. Our world had become about survival. Outwardly I was fine, with each new move I made new friends and at school I was a high achiever, but inwardly I felt a deep sadness. My heart was longing for connection and stability, yet my entire world was unstable.

In my early adolescent years, the inner turmoil sought to destroy me with feelings of not wanting to live, alcohol and substances to numb the emotional pain and boys to feel loved, but love was not my reality. From a young adolescent, I faced several dark moments of violation, which resulted in compounding trauma. Not that I blame myself, but the deep sense of unworthiness within me was like a magnet to danger. One particular day was the single most terrifying day of my life. This raped me further of my sense of self-worth, impacting my desire to live. My life had become driven by extreme fear; fear that gripped my mind day and night. In my search for security, love and belonging my next steps turned further into darkness, finding myself in a violent and coercive relationship with a man 10 years older than me. Fear increasingly became my companion and survival was my reward. I was merely eighteen.

Out of darkness though also comes hope. In that same year, my heart was gifted with love, purpose, and hope for a new future; I was pregnant. This became the beginning of the most powerful turning point in my life. The love I felt for my baby was intense, deep and powerful. I had love within me. As I am sure you could predict, however, the abusive relationship increased in intensity and fear continued to grip my innermost being. Nightmares played out like watching the same movie over and over. Trepidation and anxiety consumed me daily as the coercive control increased.

I was always on the lookout for when the next rage would erupt. Living in fear and unpredictability led me to employing survival strategies to resist harm and increase safety, including learning when to surrender and conform. On one occasion, when I was seven months pregnant, I was kicked to the ground with steel cap boots. Never again did I tell him to do his own washing. In reality, my strategies for safety only reduced risk some of the time; my life was frightening on a moment by moment basis.

I knew my life would not change if I stayed in the existing reality. I would die in the violence my life was enmeshed in, where danger and death threats were real. I made many attempts to leave and found myself back in the same nightmare, but I never gave up. I was determined to find a way to make my existing reality obsolete. I had to save myself, no one else could do it for me. My life had the potential to continue down a spiral of adversity, harm and toxic stress and there was also the potential for change, so I made the most powerful decision of my life.

I chose to leave at all costs and search for the life I was truly longing for and worthy of. I was determined that his power and control would no longer control me. I took control of my life, my future, and the wellbeing of my baby. By aligning my thoughts and actions to a sense of love and purpose, I enabled my life to take on new meaning. The love in my heart for my baby was now the motivation to also love myself. I left the home I loved, my connections and my belongings. I left it all. The thought of being caught leaving was frightening, but my escape was successful. It was worth everything I lost; I had my whole life to gain.

The moment that changed everything was when I noticed the polarity between one decision and another and heard my own whisper for change. In that moment, I was determined that this was my year to walk away from harm, start living a life I loved, recognise my own self-worth, and create an amazing life. Paving out a new life was my responsibility and I had to draw on all the inner strength and bravery I could find. So I chose to be courageous, I chose to be brave. Embracing a shift in my mindset and lifestyle changed everything. It changed my relationships, wellbeing, happiness, ability to provide a safe family home, career opportunities, and my future.

Most importantly, it changed how I perceived myself. By making a stand and saying no to violence in my life, I was saying yes to being worthy of so much more. It also changed my baby's life. Transformation always creates a ripple effect.

I had already been laying the foundations for my new life, without realising it. Pregnancy and motherhood changed the way I embraced life, focusing on health and wellbeing by nourishing my body, mind, and soul. I had begun writing pages (and pages!) of inspirational words; poetry; self-affirmations about being loved and protected, and journaling my feelings, thoughts, dreams and hopes for my future. Expressing myself through the power of writing became a way of releasing embodied emotions and a powerful part of my healing. I now write to inspire others. My spirituality gave me an inner assurance and strength that everything would be ok. It is without a doubt, what preserved my life. I was on a life changing journey and beginning to realise that my life could be one that I wanted to live.

It was not easy though, I stayed in multiple places during the first year in search of safety. It felt like danger was following me. In healing from the trauma experiences, part of my challenge was to not only be safe, but to feel safe. My survival brain had been switched to full strength for so long, it took time to turn the dial down. With trust broken multiple times, I developed an incredible inner alarm system, amazing at noticing danger cues in order to develop powerful protective strategies. What I also needed was to learn to trust myself and my environment again. I was starting my life over, which meant finding a new place to live and making new connections. The more I was able to establish my new life from a position of safety, the more my internal magnet for danger lowered.

There have been many challenges along the way, in both my personal and professional life, challenges which also provided opportunities for powerful breakthroughs. My life experiences gave me insight into the ways in which adversity affects thought processes and behaviours, how emotional imprints become suppressed within our unconscious mind and how trauma becomes embodied. It also gave me insight into the potential that exists for change. The years of adverse experiences became my strength, giving me empathy and passion to have influence in the world. Instilled within me is a deep knowing that transformational power exists within all of us, the universe watches over us and there is always hope and opportunity to create a new life path, no matter what we experience in life.

The setbacks in my life provided the foundation for post-traumatic growth and transformational influence. Standing up for the rights of children and young people to live free from violence and abuse, and supported to reach their full potential, became my passion. For over 30 years my commitment to child protection has been tenacious, impacting the lives of hundreds of children, young people, and their families to transform their reality from trauma, adversity, risk of harm and poor outcomes, to connection, belonging, safety and wellbeing.

My professional journey has been exceptionally rewarding, although it has not always been easy navigating the trauma and harm some people have experienced. There were times where I felt emotionally overwhelmed, not wanting to hear any more stories of harm. One particular day, when the sad stories seemed too much, I contemplated whether it was time to walk away. I also reflected on how walking away from working in the area of child harm does not change the fact that harm exists. The process of reflection led me to being even more inspired to make a difference in the world and my passion for preventing harm outweighed my feelings of overwhelm. Over the years I have learnt to balance my emotions and navigate stories of trauma and harm, through conscious and reflective practice, holistic wellbeing, and self-care strategies.

Over the years I provided social work services to pregnant teenagers, young mothers, children at risk, families needing intensive support and ran a range of community programs. I supported families to embrace a better way of living and take action to establish healthy and safe connections. A young 17 year old mother often comes into my thoughts. Being at significant risk of having her newborn baby removed by child protection services, we put a plan in place for developing parenting skills, securing safe accommodation, and accessing community support. Focusing on being the mother she wanted to be meant there was no valid reason to have her baby taken from her. The outcomes for her and her baby could have been far different; the decisions made at that time changed everything. This story is not unlike other young mothers I have supported.

My passion increased from an individual context to impacting at wider community, national and international levels. I have provided leadership and consulting to hundreds of services across Australia and New Zealand, developing child protection policy and training professionals in child protection, complex trauma, and reflective practice. My mission has been expansive, training services across health, education, child disability, out of home care, family support, sports, businesses, and local councils.

I led New Zealand's National Violence Intervention Programme across community, hospital and primary health services to being a leader in the country. In this role I set up systems, formed key partnerships, trained health professionals, and created clinical processes and resources. Alongside this, I led a campaign for child protection legislative change, advocating for child protection policies and training to be legally mandated. It took four years of advocacy before coming to fruition. Underpinning the success in these areas of work, was my hope to prevent further harm towards children and young people, save children's lives from maltreatment and increase safety and wellbeing.

More recently, I have developed quality improvement processes for services working in the area of child trauma and child protection, implementing a framework across multiple Queensland services. Aligned with my purpose to increase child wellbeing, projects have focused on applying a trauma-informed and developmental lens to engaging effectively with children and young people at risk of harm. The process has enhanced the way practitioners approach child focused practice, setting intentions for connection and engagement. Making an impact through listening to and validating stories; acknowledging worries, hopes and dreams; supporting child development; and establishing safe pathways where needed, created the opportunity for life changing outcomes.

My life journey, educational background and professional expertise has meant more children have had their voices heard and their lives changed. Although it has not always been easy navigating my own emotions with the trauma stories of others, it has given me a deep passion for preventing harm and increasing wellbeing in the lives of children, young people, and families. My commitment to child and family wellbeing and protection was born through my own experiences. These experiences provided opportunities for lessons, transformation and growth and form the basis of my passion today and my steps moving forward. As I stay true to my heart and soul's purpose and continue to pave new pathways, there is an incredible opportunity for continued impact.

By starting my own consulting and training business, to inspire even more change in people's lives, my passion is to enhance service delivery through transformative training, implementation of a Conscious Practice Framework and resources to inspire change. I have noticed over the years that services often define people by their dysfunction, rather than by their true value. Sometimes potential hides under layers of self-protection, emotional overwhelm and wavering mental health, but potential for change exists in everyone.

Working alongside people who have experienced trauma, complexity and harm requires a deeper level of reflective and conscious practice, drawing on neuroscience, spirituality, and clearly defined goals. When practitioners align their purpose with trauma-transformative principles, their practice becomes more intentional, meaningful, and life-changing. Services can only be transformative to the extent in which they raise the expectation for true change in people's lives and inspire new patterns of thinking, living and being. By shifting professional perceptions, the possibility of achieving optimal client outcomes increases.

From personal experience, working with complexity can be emotionally challenging. When practitioners have a deep awareness of their own conscious and unconscious processes, practice can go beyond trauma-informed care to trauma-transformative. As all practitioners experience emotional overwhelm at some point, and many have their own trauma histories, there is a pressing need for alignment between the personal and professional context, increasing mental, emotional, and psychological wellbeing. Increasing practitioner wellness, by running practitioner workshops and retreats for rejuvenation, celebration, forming aligned connections, skill building and allowing space to express the language of the heart and soul, will enhance their client work.

I have spoken internationally on topics covered in my story, including complex trauma, child and family safety, professional wellbeing and trauma-transformative practice. I am passionate about inspiring change at organisational, practice and community levels and speaking provides the opportunity for impact across these contexts. As community attitudes minimise the widespread effects of harm on individuals and families, the wider community needs to gain a deeper understanding.

Conferences I have spoken at include International Mental Health, Child Safe Organisations, Frontline Mental Health, Stop Domestic and Family Violence, Step up for Children, Children in Crisis, and Youth Health. For me, speaking brings the personal and professional context together. Behind every speaker is a story and a passion to impart new ways of thinking and being. I would love to be invited to your next event or meeting to share more on these themes and can be contacted via the links provided.

My hope is that my story inspires you to increase your expectation that, no matter what adverse experiences have occurred in people's lives, new pathways can be created, life trajectories can be changed, and lives can be transformed. By increasing belief that post-traumatic growth and transformative living is possible for all, practitioners can set their intentions to achieve optimal and life changing outcomes for themselves and their clients. Individuals and families can be guided and inspired to change and transform their lives, by drawing on neuroscience, spirituality, creating mindset changes, aligning their actions with their goals and purpose, and embracing the transformational opportunity that lies within hope and courage.

"Our higher self is always calling us to a more inspired life. We are only ever a moment away from creating a whole new reality, where one decision can change everything."

About the Author

Nikki is the founder of Nikki Butler Consulting. Born in New Zealand, living in Queensland, Australia. She is a Child Protection Consultant, Transformational Trainer, International Speaker, and Instructional Designer, with qualifications in social work, philosophy, and professional supervision.

Speaking internationally and training services in child health, trauma-transformation, conscious practice, child and family protection and practitioner wellbeing, Nikki has been influential in increasing the safety, wellbeing and happiness of hundreds of children, young people, and their families.

Nikki has featured in the New Zealand Herald, Radio New Zealand, The Social Work Now Journal and received a Queensland Child Safe Organisations award. Nikki loves to study the connection between the mind, body and spirit and is inspired by being in nature.

Email: nikki@nikkibutler.com.au
Instagram/Facebook: @nikkibutler_consultant
Website: https://nikkibutler.com.au

Taku Cooper

What advice would you give your younger self?

The question in the Facebook post was *'If you could give advice to your younger self, what would you say?'* Some of the comments were the normal cliches, 'Follow your dreams', 'Don't let others dim your light', 'You got this'. Others were more personal.

I don't usually comment on things like this but today I stood for a long while with my finger poised over the comment box. I tapped a few letters then deleted them. Tapped; deleted again.

I wanted to write something profound, but instead of profundity, my finger trembled. A hollowness filled my head, always a precursor of some inner realisation needing to be examined. I closed my eyes against the noise, accompanied by sudden waves of emotion rolling up from my belly. Breathe, Taku, breathe. It's only a Facebook post.

Opening my eyes, I looked down and there she stood as clear as day. Her bowl-shaped haircut with a mullet was the pride of many mum hairdressers in the 70s. She had one missing front tooth; the others in danger of being bucked due to thumb sucking. Her feet were bare because shoes were for school. A red and white striped jumper topped purple pants with a Chinese girls print. The familiarity of her second-hand clothes added fuel to the fire of my guilt.

The 6-year-old face with the large brown eyes that were also mine, shined expectantly at me.

"So," she asked, an excited smile lighting her face, hands clasped to her chest. "How did we do? Did we live all of our dreams? Where do we live? What do we do? Am I a police woman? Or a famous author?" Bouncing up and down with each question.

Standing in the middle of the Helensvale Westfield on a busy Sunday morning I started to cry. Glad to be wearing my ear pods, giving an impression I was crying to someone and not about the hazy mirage of my yesterdays. My crying was not gentle; it was the kind that comes with heavy lumps sticking in your chest. Crying that should have been shed in stages, not saved up for one huge explosion.

The last thing I wanted to tell her, or anyone, was that a series of immature decisions I had dressed up as 'being adventurous', had made us homeless and fast approaching broke. Again. The job we had loved for 6 years had been redefined due to current global circumstances. We were overweight, inflamed, sad, single, and 54. I had done a lot of stupid things, caused many people great pain and I hadn't amounted to much at all. As far as I was concerned, our life sucked and I was scared. Properly scared. Scared of not only of what the future held, but scared to tell her I had failed her, failed as a person, a mother and a human being. I didn't want to answer her questions, because to do that would mean that I would have to examine my own beliefs and face my own shortcomings. I would have to admit to myself that I was a monumental failure. Instead, I stumbled out to my car, trying to find respite. On the drive back to my house-sit, my mind rudely catapulted me back to my childhood.

When I was 6, I would hide behind my father's garage reading fairy tales, sucking my thumb and daydreaming. I hid from a father whose violence was unpredictable and terrifying. Sitting around doing nothing was enough to cause his anger and loosen his belt. Reading stories meant I could escape to do anything and everything. My dreams weren't confined to Hans Christian Anderson. I also wanted to do everything everyone else did. When I went to the Post Office, I was the postie. At the bank, I was the teller. At school, I was the teacher. On television I was a policewoman like Angie Dickinson, and I wrote books in a treehouse in Africa like Willard Price. I wanted to travel to all the places I read about and live in an apartment on the beach in Australia where net curtains billowed over my bed in the sea breeze. After school, I'd hurry to the local furniture shop to get their monthly catalogue, rushing home to sit behind the garage, carefully choosing one item from each page to put into my future apartment. Then I would write about it. Head in the clouds. At that age, it was just a matter of survival and dreaming. Life continues to march on, responsibility sets in and sometimes reality knocks really hard. Yet life continues anyway.

I denied her audience on that Westfield day and many more days after. She appeared at the oddest times, sitting quietly beside me as I mindlessly watched reality renovation shows on my phone, wishing my life away. I would catch her in the corner of my eye in the passenger seat of the car staring out the window, sucking her thumb. Or next to me on the train. She never made eye contact with me, or rather, I never made eye contact with her. The day our relationship changed; I had caught a glimpse of her in the park staring curiously at the lorikeets roosting in the trees. Her form being made diminutive by the tall trees made me cry again.

That same night I succumbed to a particularly nasty bout of tonsillitis forcing me to be bedridden for almost a week. In my fevered state my dreams were wildly varied and amazingly vivid. In one I was standing on a mountain ridge holding hands with her exactly as she was in Westfield. Smiling encouragingly, she turned her head to look along the ridge. I gazed down an infinite line of people who all felt like me astonished to see my mother further down the ridge. Stunned, I looked in the other direction and could see another infinite line of people who also felt like me. I was startled to see my own daughter in that line. We were all holding hands, linked forever. I looked down at the child of me and understood this was the line of all the versions of the souls I had ever been and all the souls I was ever going to be. Tears welled again and I knew without a doubt that she and I had to talk. We were inextricably linked in this eternal Generational Line.

As I slept through dreams, falling in and out of fevers, she came and went as well. We talked. Eventually, she asked questions as we both sat cross legged in my own mind. My head hung down, too ashamed to face her and admit I'd blown it.

"Did we work at the Post Office?" Was the first question she asked me.

I answered quietly. "Yes, we did."

She clapped and smiled.

"Did we work in a bank?" The question was breathless with excitement.

"Ah, yes we did." It was only for a short while but we did do that, I thought.

"Did we be a teacher?"

"Not a school teacher but we taught swimming and classes about running and fitness," I answered. "So yes, we were a teacher."

"So, we can swim? And run?" Her voice pitched to a squeak.

"Yes, we are really good at both of those things." I recalled how we were terrified of the water and would death grip the side of the school pool for the entire season. And running? Well, we were a little bit fat for that back then, but we eventually ran marathons.

She was bug eyed as she mouthed WOW.

"Have we gone on adventures and travelled to far away countries?"

It was at that point that my head jerked up as I recalled the travelling, we had done. The bungy jumping, camel riding, abseiling, snorkelling, free diving, marathon running, triathloning, deep sea fishing, whale swimming, big mountain climbing and wide country cycling. I thought about the food in the Pacific Islands and Asia, the vastness of USA, the beauty of travelling our home country of New Zealand, learning some of the language of New Caledonia and East Timor, of settling in Australia and travelling this country too.

"WE LIVE IN AUSTRALIA?" She practically screamed in delight. "WE LIVE IN AUSTRALIA?"

I actually laughed out loud as I nodded. "Yes, we do. Those were lorikeets you were watching the other day in the trees."

"Lorikeets? Not parrots. Lorikeets. Oh my god. Did we write a book?" She clapped in delight.

"Yes, we did but it wasn't in the treetops of Africa." I paused, an amazing realisation beginning to overwhelm me. "Actually, we wrote in an apartment on the beach," visualising the times the wind would blow the net curtain all over the place and how it annoyed me when it did. I thought she might faint when she saw that.

She breathed hard, before she lisped "Did we become a police officer like Angie Dickinson?"

I laughed again, "Um, as a matter of fact yes, we did. We don't do that anymore, but yes, we absolutely did."

Her face was agog, her eyes like saucers. We shared an elated understanding that she had set the goals for our life when she was 6 and over the next 48 years we had achieved all of them and then some.

Together we now sat beaming at each other, her face in raptures as she witnessed my memories, astounded that we had also become a mother which hadn't been on our minds way back then. For her, our life was a success and we still had several decades to go. It could only get better right?

The expression on her face changed from elation to bewilderment then crumpled. Anxiously I knew the next question was the one question I didn't want to answer. This was the question that meant I would have to dissect, inspect and justify the beliefs I had learned from others.

Tears filled her eyes, her bottom lip stuck out, quivering. "We did everything we said we would do. Why are we so unhappy? Why do you hate me and call me nasty names?" she sobbed. "What did I do that was so bad?"

She disappeared. Sobbing and bereft, I lay in bed, miserable with my sore throat, my throbbing head and the failed obligation to a little girl who had depended on me since we were 6 to feel safe and treasured. Never mind the goals we had smashed.

I had spent decades chastising and berating myself for all that I thought I wasn't. I had allowed myself to be bullied, to be hurt, to be beaten. I had treated myself as though I had no worth, making poor choices that not only damaged me physically, emotionally and spiritually, but my pain caused pain to others. What I had not counted on was that in my actions, I had allowed THAT little girl to be damaged. I had thoughtlessly hurt her. Not once had I stopped to acknowledge all the amazing things we had seen and done, had never made her feel okay about who she was, about where she was going, about the decisions we were making. For her entire life I had punished her over and over.

I cried, slept and apologised. I cried, slept and promised. I cried, slept and forgave. I cried, slept and began healing.

Within the tears, I unpacked many of my behaviours, realising they were partly driven by the violent experiences we had endured through our childhood and into our adult life. Things we had no control over, yet tragically sought out just to feel noticed. Damaging beliefs were the result of this violence, beliefs that formed my self-destructive opinion of myself.

Finally, I got honest. I admitted my fears of ageing and not having a stable life to retire into. I admitted my limiting financial habits and my unhealthy obsession with food. I had a fear of relationships with men, and an inability to trust others. I admitted that no matter how well I performed, I never felt I was good enough, having to continually strive for approval. I recognised that no amount of external approval was ever going to help because I felt I didn't deserve it. I told her I was sorry and would vow to do so much better. I told her all of the things I wished I hadn't done as we were going along. There were goals I still wished to attain and now it was too late. I was done.

She asked very simply, "Why are we done? We have time to do those things don't we?"

As silly as this may sound, I hadn't thought about it that way. We did have time to do those things. After 5 days in bed, I finally got out, showered, dressed and walked down the road to a café.

I was hungry. For food and for change. She walked with me, taking in everything and asking dozens of questions.

Over the next few weeks, she was my regular companion, showing me the beauty and excitement of a life that I had regarded as mediocre. She marvelled at the car we drove, the huge shopping centres and the clothes we wore. Delighted in riding the tram and the train. Sitting in my office gaping in wonder at the machinery constructing the building across the road. The foods we ate were the most delicious, and city life was beyond exciting. Birds, flowers and the Australian bush rendered her speechless. Everything we did was a marvel to her. Soon, I found myself caught up in perceiving my world through someone else's eyes, a tourist in my own life, an observer who wants only to see the good in us. What I considered a failed life, she decided was amazing, exciting, and with endless possibilities. Through her I learned that I was worth more than I could ever have expected and what I had accomplished so far was nothing short of miraculous.

As I continued to travel my life through her eyes, I began moving down the long road to healing the pain I had caused us. She taught me to honour who I am as a person and a human and to find all the value that I deserved in the actions I took.

I made many resolutions with her. I resolved to not belittle myself, as that belittles every version of us, past and present. I resolved to have patience with the process and to treat every experience like it was the first time. I vowed to congratulate myself for a job well done whilst seeking new experiences with an open mind. She and I set several more years of plans and this time I knew it would be different. It was now incumbent upon me to approach the coming decades with absolute optimism, to know that my opinion of myself and my activities was far more essential than what anyone else thought of me.

Months passed and our lives merged back into one. I couldn't do all the work I needed without help so I also sought assistance from many teachers but notably from a talented Naturopath to improve my foundational physical health, a Theta Practitioner and a psychologist to help piece us back together. My focus was to heal us as we continued to grow into the woman I am today.

I consciously remind myself to take each day as it comes and to remember to find the beauty in what we are doing. I relish being my biggest cheerleader as I positively influence myself. There are times when I fall back into old debilitating habits. I catch myself singing in public, or being too enthusiastic or wearing clothes of a woman a decade younger than me, times where I feel disgusted with what I eat. I unkindly call myself stupid or immature. She reappears, sitting off to the side reminding me that what I say is falling heavily on the one who finds all of my life a gift from God.

Almost a year later, her visits are rare. I have embarked on a new journey of achieving new goals and dreams we decided to pursue during that week of illness. These days, I am filled with gratitude for the ability to connect with my child-self. She came at the perfect moment to remind me that my responsibility was to her, to myself and to the many versions of me that are yet to come. Generational healing has to start somewhere and it has started with me. It was so powerful to have her tell me that she is incredibly proud of me, that she approves of the life we have led and the life we are yet to create. She loves me in all of my imperfectly perfect ways.

And because she is me, then it is with humility and a state of wonder that I can now declare that I too am proud of me. I approve of me and I love me so much my heart aches with joy. When I am in need to a reality check, I can call her to me and she will come. Because she is me and through her I am learning faith, hope and courage.

Thank you, 6-year-old Taku. You saved my life xx

About the Author

Taku works in law enforcement and is the author of the novel 'In The Beginning' a story of a girl navigating her way through trauma with the help of spirit guides.

She's also a qualified personal trainer, certified as a Science of Stretching instructor, Theta Healer, and a talented Oracle Card reader, giving insights in a fun yet thought provoking way.

Navigating out of a self-destructive life into generational healing has proven to be a subject she feels she can easily relate to in others.

Although not an expert, Taku believes we can gain a lot of clarity speaking to those who have experienced trauma and moved through it. There is hope. Taku is looking forward to writing her second novel.

Email: TakuKCooper@gmail.com
Facebook: https://www.facebook.com/takucooperstoryteller/

Natalie Curtis

This is not Love

It was approaching the summer of 2012, and London was hosting the Olympic and Paralympic games, I look back at the incredible memories of working on the build of the games, the excitement was unreal, and I had managed to get tickets to one of the greatest games ever for both via the public ballot. I had worked for several years on 2 projects on the park, I had seen and been part of the incredible work all the projects had put into making this the greatest games to date.

I loved and still love my career choice as a Health and Safety professional, the lows and highs of working on such prestigious projects is something I feel very proud of, it's a long standing joke with my work colleagues "did you work on the Olympic and Paralympic build" because I still talk about it to this day, the best project I have worked on and I have been lucky to work on a lot of incredible projects but London 2012 will always have a special place in my heart.

Despite such incredible memories of 2012 and all the emotions that I was experiencing, I was hiding a difficult "behind closed doors" issue that was really starting to affect my physical and mental well-being, I had entered into a relationship that was already exhausting, taking every bit of me as "Natalie" a happy bubbly person who strived to be positive and help others. I couldn't live as I had previously, I was being called constantly on my mobile or facetimed throughout to check where I was, I was quizzed about who I spoke to and where I was, what you doing or what are you eating, my property was being damaged or smashed up in his rages, the shouting and screaming at me was terrifying, I missed events but not because I was told you can't go that the direct manner, it was made so difficult due to fear and abuse that it was easier to not go and manage the perpetrators expectations than have a normal happy life. It was then that I was experiencing Domestic abuse, it took until the summer of 2018 to leave my then husband.

I was trapped, unable to explain to others including friends and family what I was experiencing because often the abuse would seem subtle, not that big of a deal, or the feeling of did that really happen and then convincing your brain that it can't be that bad, you replay every single episode of abuse, even justify and lie about it because why would someone who "loves" you treat you this way but these periods would pass and he would attempt to appease me with gifts and promises to change his behaviour.

These episodes escalated and escalated, I was living in constant fear of my life, because the perpetrators will tell you exactly what is going to happen to you if you leave them, a lot of "fears" were becoming an everyday reality, I felt I would never be believed, how can I explain to someone the everyday torture you are living under, because the answer I couldn't hear was "just leave", that was not an option in my mind, I wanted the abuse to stop. I wanted to leave so many times, to the point where I wasn't going to burden anyone with my problems, I will just run away, hoping that I will not be found because I couldn't go back home, a place where we should and be able to be safe. With threats of constant violence that then turned into reality I was a victim, a victim that was so unhappy, scared, mentally and physically unwell, a broken bone, constant bruises, drained, and suffering from anxiety, I become a recluse in my own home.

I had no money, despite working full-time and working overtime. I was financially destitute, in so much debt that my ex-perpetrator had put all bills in my name, took out loans in my name, took out car finance in my name, I couldn't even afford to get to work. How can I just leave? I was trapped with my abuser. Living daily on eggshells waiting for the next episode of abuse.

The lead up to me making the decision to finally leave for good, I was unable to piece together normal day to day life activities, those simple everyday tasks were beyond difficult even down to having a shower – it would sometimes take me an hour to go from my bedroom to the bathroom, I would physically shake in fear from head to foot. Not safe at home and not safe leaving home and not safe at work, he worked on the same projects I did as a sub-contractor.

I wrote several diary entries on my phone – He comments about double suicide is the only way out for us, I can't take this, how I'm still going I will never know, the abuse continues every single day, it's always my fault never his, various times I go to call 999 as I fear for my life, I have just not had the strength. I know it will come one day.

He chased me around the apartment with a knife held in his hand, I'm just going to kill you now, I begged and begged for him not to stab me, I remained calm but inside I was in complete panic mode, the thought of being stabbed took me to rock bottom.

My wedding and engagement rings were pawned a month prior to me leaving, he dragged me to the pawn shop and said we need money, and this was the only option, at this point I was building the strength and courage to leave, I had exhausted every other avenue. This is not love, this is spiteful and hurtful, I felt this gave me the start of real hope that I'm leaving for good, I had many other attempts prior. Why did you marry him a question I had constantly on replay in my head, fear, I never booked our wedding, he did, seems like that's a caring, "showing of interest" kind of guy? He told my mum prior to me that he booked the wedding date as a "surprise" for me.

My brother and sister-in-law announced that she was pregnant, and it was going to be a little girl! A glimmer of hope rushed through me, this was my focus, this is my saviour, I held on to hope that I can do this, the fear of not meeting her gave me a purpose to leave. These moments of hope were starting to pull me through.

On Saturday 30th June 2018 – I fled with just the clothes on my back, with the hope that this new journey a life where I can live abuse free took it's first steps. I called a friend to pick me up, I didn't feel ok to drive, I was up all night being sick, shaking and in fear of what to do next but determined to never return to a life of abuse or worse being murdered.

Later that day I went to a family BBQ and told close family members exactly what I was going through, my mum knew something was seriously wrong in our marriage but every time she asked questions I would lie or close the conversation down, friends also had their suspicions but again I would close the conversation down. It was the biggest relief to talk to family although my journey has been an education to all friends and family, I was believed.

My mum asked quietly so what do you want to do next? Come home and stay with us, we will do whatever it takes to support you. I moved back to my parents, a space I knew that I would be cared for and loved, but the fear that it might not be a safe place because I had been back before but this time it was different, this time it was for good.

I had previously called the police he was arrested and charged in 2017 for threats to kill me but under the malicious communications law, I never had a space to talk to the police about what was really happening in my life. In fact, I had the police asking for me to support him as some people go through tough periods in their life, I was also victim blamed. I felt a burden on them but also the feeling of exhaustion that they don't understand domestic abuse.

I visited my GP where I was diagnosed with anxiety and depression, I was never asked about my home life.

Even when I sustained a fractured femur from one of his violent episodes, I was never allowed to see the consultants alone, he spoke on my behalf. It took months to recover, the abuse got worse as I was unable to move, drive, or go to work, I had to rest for 3 months at home. A perpetrators ideal scenario, but me, Natalie, a victim's continued living nightmare.

On Sunday 1st July 2018 after constant messages and calls from the perpetrator telling me to come home and that he wants to change and that he will book in (again) with his therapist and psychiatrist to get better I called the police on the non-emergency number, my gut feeling that I have constantly ignored was getting louder and I feared for the safety of my family and I.

I recall saying to the police operator please help, I don't want to be another statistic, he asked me to describe what I meant, I gave as much detail as I could remember and piece together, I had a meeting with police the next day and further worked with the police for 3 weeks giving every detail and account of my life of domestic abuse, the officers were incredible, they listened, they believed me and they supported me throughout the investigation. They were trained in Domestic Abuse, and I believe this made a huge impact on their response in presenting the case to the CPS. The Police signposted me to Women's Aid for specialist support and gave me the confidence to reach out to them.

On reflection I now would advise victims and survivors to contact your local Domestic Abuse specialists prior to leaving as a safety plan would have been implemented, I now know it's the most dangerous time for victims when they leave, the risk is even greater.

An arrest and charge were authorised in July 2018. Also, he was held in remand until the court hearing, I had space, I had some time to put me first. I had a list that continued forever of things I needed to complete; it was completely overwhelming. Some days I ticked off a couple of things other days I physically couldn't get enough energy together to get out of bed let alone look at the "to do" list, I felt even more of a failure.

My ex-perpetrator was sentenced in October 2018 to a 2-year prison sentence and made subject to an indefinite restraining order for Controlling & Coercive Behaviour.

I was so embarrassed and ashamed that I just wanted to stay indoors, in fact I would go out when it was dark so no one could see me.

Making the call to Women's Aid and talking to a stranger about my life was by no means easy.

From my first appointment with Women's aid I knew that my life was about to head in the right direction, although I was scared, upset and talking to a case worker that I have never met before I was ready to talk openly about my experience of domestic abuse, I was ready to live free from abuse, I deserved to live a happy normal life, I repeatedly told myself.

The abuse was chipping away at me, my confidence, my self-esteem, " you are a waste of space" "you are useless" "you will never find someone who loves you like I do" "you are mental – you need medication" constantly sounding in my mind, If I cried I was told " stop crying you are making me more angry" If I never showed emotion because I was petrified I was told I don't care about our relationship" If my ex preparator thought I was going to leave, I was told "I'm going to Kill myself and it's your fault" That stress and guilt alone was horrific.

I walked in broken, I attended the Freedom Programme, empower programme and specialist trauma counselling, I felt like this journey is continuing to head in the right direction, I still undergo therapy when required, and the shame I originally felt no longer lives within me.

I deserve the advice and support that is available. I've "rewired" my brain to now accept none of this way my fault, the shame is with those of perpetrating Domestic Abuse.

I was prepared to start again, rebuild my life, material things can be replaced in the future I reminded myself every day, my health and wellbeing is now my top priority and continues to be, I'm not perfect at it but realign to put time aside for me.

To know I have helped thousands of others who are experiencing Domestic Abuse was my only reason for me to speak out publicly. I wanted to help other victims and survivors know they are not alone. We must look at the devastating statistics here in the UK and around the world to understand why Domestic Abuse is everyone's business.

My employer was very supportive, I was determined to work with my employer to ensure others know where to go for help and support I'm the founder and co-chair of the Domestic Abuse working group and the work we have been continuously doing since 2019 is now being spoken about as industry leading which is beyond incredible, to reflect on a journey since 2018, my freedom year, of the continued opportunities to help others victim/survivors I will continue to share my journey with the world, the mission continues to be invited to speak at different events expanding globally so I can continue to drive change.

I continue to help others complete the gaps of the missing jigsaw, from sharing my journey and working alongside the Domestic Abuse sector on who to contact and who specialises in what area to court cases both family and criminal, navigating through the criminal justice system is difficult and confusing, to speaking at events and working alongside police forces who want to help victims and survivors, we have a long way to go but by everyone helping end the stigma and shame around Domestic Abuse, we are making a huge difference to lives of others. Ask yourself a question – are you doing enough? Do you know your local Domestic Abuse services? Would you know what to do if someone you work with, or a family member was disclosed to you?

Talking out about Domestic Abuse is never easy, it's upsetting, triggering and can sometimes require you to take a step back to recharge but the new friendships that I have formed with other survivors is beyond incredible, there is a very special connection between survivors, their strength is powerful and inspiring, and I'm constantly being educated, knowledge is power.

Out of really tough times I constantly reflect on the good memories that I make and continue to make a few of my highlights are walking the Catwalk with the incredible, inspiring survivor sister Mel B (Spice girls) for a special fundraising night for Women's Aid, ironically my worst fear is "centre of attention" but I lived in the moment and enjoyed every second of the event, oh and yes I so wanted to run around signing Spice Girls songs as I'm a huge fan of them. I couldn't believe I had been paired with Melanie, what an absolute honour and start of our continued friendship. I still look at the pictures and videos thinking wow that is me!

Women's Aid asked me if I would like to talk about my journey with the producers and cast of a very popular TV soap in the UK, Eastenders, this is seen by millions of viewers, reaching a new audience, and educating the viewers on Domestic Abuse was an incredible opportunity. The messages and comments were really overwhelming but vital viewing as many victims / survivors like myself do not realise you're experiencing domestic abuse, it's hard to label domestic abuse as that when you are living it. It's a crime and has devastating affects not only of the victim but for your family and friends too.

I'm grateful for my social media platforms, where this journey started on speaking out, I love to work with employers who want to make a change in their organisations to help support victims of domestic abuse, knowing that it will help someone else, I would love the take this further and explore what influences I can make all over the world.

At the absolute heart of Domestic Abuse sits Controlling and Coercive Behaviour, everyone experiences different behaviours and different levels, but the fundamentals are textbook. This is a law that is not currently throughout the world, but it absolutely needs to be. We must do more as individuals to ensure others experiencing domestic abuse know where to get help and support. Specialist Domestic Abuse services are hugely underfunded here in the UK and throughout the world, I feel like it's my calling to be a part of the change.

It's not acceptable to live in fear of your life and there is never an excuse for this behaviour, ever. It does not get better, it gets worse, the control tightens.

Together we can make a difference and that difference to victims and survivors is life changing and in some circumstances lifesaving.

About the Author

Natalie is a proud Survivor Ambassador with Women's Aid and EIDA who continues to raise awareness of the devastating impact of experiencing Domestic Abuse.

In 2018 Natalie fled her marital home with just the clothes on her back, determined to rebuild her life after her ex-perpetrator was the first to be jailed in the UK for Controlling & Coercive behaviour.

Sharing her journey and featuring on many media outlets BBC Documentary - Is this Coercive Control, MTV Mia Boardman – Domestic Violence and Me, The Sun, Guardian, The Independent, The Telegraph, to help others is a passion she drives for change.

Natalie loves spending time with her friends and family.

Twitter: @Natsc2012
Email: youarenotalone.natalie@gmail.com

Maree Delaney

Hijacked by my failing health... or rather rescued by it.

Leaning back into my seat, the warmth of the morning sun on my skin, a crisp but gentle breeze against my face, surrounded by the harmonic sounds of crashing ocean waves. I could taste the salty air on my lips... This is my early morning happy place and only a stone's throw from my home.

H O N K.... an ear-piercing blast gave me a reality check, the horn from the excavator my indicator that I was fully loaded. Unconsciously my mind had wandered off and I was reminiscing about my former coastal life. The stark reality now 800 kilometres from my beloved Sunshine Coast, in a dusty, dirty coal mine in Central Australia, starting over.

Let me paint a picture for you, I am clad head to toe in the cliche orange hi-vis attire, tinted safety glasses pressed against my face and my steel cap boots laced up my shins. I took immense pride and joy in operating dump truck 31, a vibrant egg yolk yellow beast. As one of two females in this predominantly male workforce, surviving each day by blending in, holding my tough girl card close to my chest and rebuilding the lives of both my son and me, load by load.

Though only in my early 30's I had left behind an aspiring clothing label, a long-term relationship, a photography business and not to mention a circle of close friends. If I am totally honest on the inside I am shattered, totally unfulfilled and on the verge of burnout. The long days were unforgiving, particularly when raising a child solo and exacerbating my failing health. The conundrum.... I am bringing home a good consistent wage, more than I have ever earned as a solo mum albeit at the expense of my sanity.

Have you ever felt like this? Most of us would say "Hell Yes, that's me every day!"

Working tirelessly at a job or pursuing a struggling side hustle that has absolutely no reward outside of finances, even worse you're not getting the recognition for your efforts and most likely feeling that you are just another number on the books.

You know deep down that you are destined for more, but finding the path to embark on your next chapter seems elusive. Allow me to share with you what I have discovered—a way to reignite my inner spark and let my true magic shine.

Like music to my ears, a loud voice broke the silence "Last loads, head for lunch and the cake in the fridge, help yourself" crackling from the two-way radio mounted on my dash. There was some enthusiastic banter between the truckies about who's going to eat who's slice or who should probably skip the cake completely. Let's say it helps to have a thick skin in this industry.

Being the first to return to the parking area, I shut down my truck and enjoyed a few minutes of silence. No two-way radio chatter, no engine noise, no vibrations rattling through my aching body, not a soul in sight. It was just me with my thoughts and anticipation of planning the upcoming days off with my son.

Stepping out of the truck cabin onto the landing deck, the view from here was always picturesque (especially at dusk). In the foreground the sun's rays shimmered off the water filled dams as a group of kangaroos bound across the farmland that stretched as far as the eye could see. I paused for a moment, capturing this personal snapshot in my mind and reminding myself to keep going.

Squatting down I reached for the isolation switch, when suddenly, a deafening BOOM reverberated through my body, as if a shotgun had been fired. This is my description for the non-existent sound, but very real and excruciating pain taking hold inside of me. Instantly I broke into a sweat, that blissful silence turned to a nightmare of internal panic. Everything around me went in slow motion, but my heart rate and thoughts sped up. I couldn't physically unfold from my crouched position; the pain was now an 11/10. My joints had seized up, leaving me stranded, I was in no man's land.

The words "EMERGENCY, EMERGENCY, EMERGENCY" were raging through my mind, but there was no way I was going to sound that ALARM! Let alone subject myself to a possible incident investigation. Instead, I focused on the safety handrail in front of me and I gripped it tightly with both hands like I was hanging on for my life. Taking a few deep breaths, inhaling through my nose and exhaling through my mouth, I braced myself for the agonising pain and used the railing as support to force my body into an upright position. My heart was now galloping out of my chest, I felt a single tear roll down my cheek. With great effort, I shuffled toward the steps and slowly made my way to the ground.

I had been keeping a big secret: a debilitating sciatica pain piercing through my buttock triggered by a herniated disc in my lower spine. Most mornings it was a struggle to just get my socks and jocks on. The constant scent of heat rub, reminiscent of my childhood days in the footy sheds during the 80's, was my new daily perfume. The neurosurgeon had advised against surgery, explaining that due to my young age I would likely need a further procedure later in life as the results wouldn't last. Delay and preservation were my best defence.

An overwhelming feeling of failure and fear washed over me. How the hell were we going to survive once our savings had run dry? Here I am 35 years young facing the real possibility of a lifelong disability pension. It felt as though all of the pain and challenges from my past life were converging like an incoming tide, lapping at my feet.

In that exact moment I knew.... I WAS DONE! THAT WAS IT! There had to be a better way to provide for my son without risking my health trading time for money. It was time to create a life of fulfilment, a life living on my terms.

Hijacked by my failing health... or rather rescued by it.

It has changed my life.... Not easy but necessary.

For some time, I had been researching my previously diagnosed inflammatory bowel disease, delving into gut health and the flow on effect of inflammation on the body, fatigue and mental wellbeing. It was an eye opener to say the least. It blew my mind to understand everything that passed through my lips could affect so much more than just the number on the scales.

Freshly unemployed, relying on savings and sheer grit, I rolled up my sleeves and got to work. Weekly appointments with physiologists and acupuncture sessions became my new normal.

Easing the pain and slowly building up strength were my new priorities. I immersed myself in seminars, workshops and specialist consultations. I had willingly supplied many bodily fluid samples for testing, some would say I almost became a human bio-hacker. Armed with test results, I developed a newly formed obsession with consuming nourishing, healthy foods suited to my specific genetic blueprint, prioritising quality over quantity always.

My thirst for knowledge continued to grow, and my ears burned with overuse from audiobooks and podcasts. Among the many mental challenges I was facing in this phase of life was a significant shift in identity. Making big changes and standing strong in my conviction whilst I had no results, no runs on the board and nothing to show for my hard work, was no easy task.

IDENTITY SHIFT = *A belief about the type of person you are being and the behaviour you will exhibit in alignment with this belief.*

From a list of many, a standout favourite book for me is "Atomic Habits" by James Clear. I have lost count how many times I have relistened to this book, adopting and integrating new behaviour and adding layers of information and knowledge each time. I urge you to take a listen or grab a hardcopy if that's more your style. I have both!

As I delved deeper into my healing journey, I threw myself into study at the Institute of Integrated Nutrition - New York.

Emerging from my studies as a lean, nearly pain free and vibrant health coach, I was ready to support others struggling with their wellbeing and guide them on a path to reclaim their health. Progress came quickly from 1:1 session's, cooking classes and workshops to a fully funded mental health community event for over 200 people.

For the first time in my working life, I felt all of my creative power, design expertise, photography skills and marketing knowledge had collided in one arena where it all just made sense. I found myself consulting with business women in the health and wellness sector. I took great pride advising, designing and elevating their brand aesthetics, imagery, events and launches. Filled with joy, I supported ambitious women to reclaim their valuable time and expand their visions and business. Amidst it all, I overlooked myself.

Universe I am ready for the next step, show me the way.

The search continued. A burning desire and persistent inkling in the back of my mind assured me that I was meant for more. A life of true freedom achieved through generating a leveraged income, that elusive saying of *"making money while you sleep"* began to resonate deeply with me. Now I know money doesn't buy you happiness firsthand, but it does provide us with choices.

Whilst I enjoyed helping others on their entrepreneurial journeys, a part of me still yearned for more. That's when I came across an Aussie mum using a smart online business model. She has created a full-time income, retired her husband and is enjoying all of what life can offer. This concept struck a chord with me and also resurrected an old, outdated belief.

Work hard, then retire at 65 when you have only got 20 years left to enjoy it.

Let's be honest that's fucking crazy!

I couldn't unsee the possibilities that were before me, I developed an itch. A new perspective began to take shape, one that opened an entirely different trajectory. In that moment I whispered to myself 'If she can do it, I can too'. Was this possible? This was my NIKE moment - Time to just do it!

Fast forward to the now. I wake up with the roosters every day, because that's my thing. There's nothing quite like brewing a fresh cup of coffee while the rest of the world sleeps. It's my sacred time, dedicated to writing my gratitude's and grounding myself before the momentum of the day kicks in. Not going to lie… it feels incredible to invest time and effort into achieving my goals and building my big vision. I bounce out of bed with purpose, armed with a crystal clear understanding that I control my own future and abundance. I still choose to work with a select range of "hell yes, you're my vibe" 1:1 and group clients, sharing my skills and experience in all things branding and design.

Meanwhile I enjoy operating a fully leveraged and automated online affiliate marketing business that complements my life and creates an additional income stream.

Deep down my desire for my family and myself is a life free from any financial limitations.

To be fully available to experience all of life's sweetness - like a piece of gluten free chocolate mud cake. Saying yes without guilt or worry of checking my bank account. Total time freedom and financial independence. Building a passive income with generational wealth and developing a powerful legacy for years to come - In my mind this is already done!

"Can't start a fire without a spark."- Bruce Springsteen

To the naked eye I look like the same old me, but I've ignited my fire and I am shining my light and walking the path for others to do the same. I am a woman with a BIG vision, an insatiable burning desire to help others who know they are meant for more, empowering them to optimise their health, escape the 9 - 5 rat race and create lives they are excited to wake up to - Lives filled with wealth, freedom and more fun than you can poke a stick at. Insert crazy dance moves here.

Hand on my heart, I am truly grateful to have the freedom to work on my own terms. I set my own hours and location of work. I am being paid to be myself, practising the ART of really living, expressing creativity and cherishing quality time with family, friends and like-minded souls. Sometimes I have to pinch myself, just to be sure that I am not dreaming.

In this very moment you too can choose to reclaim your power. You are truly magic.

You are not defined by your circumstances or past experiences. You are shaped by the desires you hold within your heart.

There is no magic pill, no secret ingredient, though adding your own spice can make things fun. It's about finding someone who is living the type of life you want and doing what they do.

Imagine wealth flowing into the hands of everyday women. There is really something magical about like-minded women coming together and collaborating. This is what lights my soul on fire. It's my mission, to show you how simple and genuinely possible it is.

I share my story with you to inspire you. It is through making courageous decisions, and embracing change that we get different results. These are the actions that change your life.

This is a friendly nudge for those stuck in the trenches with a desire for change. Take action, take the first step. Make a call, send that message or write the email. You may be hesitating, holding back or uncertain about which direction to pursue. I wholeheartedly offer my encouragement and support, as you explore the limitations of your comfort zone and venture into the unknown. Be brave, step into the *magic zone* and be open to the possibility of *abundance and transformation in your life.*

I believe in you. Take that step.

Let's create MAGIC

Always ♥ *M.A.D xxx*

About the Author

Maree is the creative leader and founder of UPLIFTED - the movement. Empowering the modern everyday goddess to build her online empire. Born in southern Victoria, then raised on the Sunshine Coast. Maree now enjoys the comforts of the Central Queensland climate and relaxed lifestyle.

Driven by a passion for creativity and a deep-rooted desire to foster a sense of community. Maree embraces the role of mentor and guide to a growing community of women who are fearlessly pursuing their passions and transforming lives.

When not sharing the high energy of her pet staffy, Maree appreciates the importance of health and wellbeing through nature, music, family and of course great coffee!

Facebook: @mareedelaney
Join her free Facebook community: **UPLIFTED** – *The Movement*
https://bit.ly/UPLIFTED-FBgroup
Instagram: @maree.a.delaney

Arwen Dyer

Intuition: the Superpower to Birthing Dreams

"Baby G" he became known, this effervescent little ray of sunshine. He was there all along: my intuitive eye saw him clearly in the invisible field of possibilities, this life waiting to grace me in the flesh. Yet the journey until our worlds collided was long and rocky. As much as I desired a sibling for my first born and as hard I tried to make it happen, the more impossible it became. The pain and longing was all encompassing: I desperately wanted this child and yet he kept escaping my grip, while I lost myself in an emotional whirlpool.

Perhaps you can relate to this, with something you desperately want? More money, a new relationship, your own home, a purposeful career you love? You are not alone, most people have at least one area of life where they desire change, where they want to manifest something else, but they keep facing blocks. Often we wonder why we experience similar circumstances over again: the same kind of relationships, a lack of finances or ongoing health concerns: this was my reality, more of the same and wondering what was wrong with me, why couldn't I have what I wanted?

The truth is we are creating our lives all of the time, and more often than not, our current reality does not match what our heart desires. Unconscious patterns and long-held beliefs keep us stuck. The topic of manifestation runs hot on social media, in spiritual circles and on the bestsellers list. Yet when life is chaotic and emotions are high, it's easy to be skeptical of manifestation… that was me.

Ambling alone along empty streets I felt black inside. I had hit rock bottom. Life as I knew it had turned upside down. I was faced with decisions that would have lasting consequences. My toddler Eider's playful ways lit up my heavy heart amidst the piles of cloth nappies, dog hair and avocado smears on the floor. It was hard to believe he was turning three. I should have been exuberant. Instead, at his party, I struggled to hold back tears, hiding behind the trees. I couldn't look my husband in the eye. Singing around Eider's requested blue mouse cake that I'd made, the best I could do was squeeze my boy tight and close.

Bearing and raising children is visceral, spiritual and intensely psychological. It's an entirety of beingness with all the rawness of life and death, flesh and blood. Parenting little ones has us experiencing a myriad of emotions and triggers all in a day. The innate power of women's bodies to germinate and birth life is beyond comprehension to me, I am in awe of nature's wild and rhythmic ways. Having a child is the birth of a matriarch: a woman who does and gives her all, suffers and carries on, and lives well beyond her limits. Here I was, like generations of mothers, obsessed about doing it all over again.

My first pregnancy and birth were a dream. Receiving my little boy at my breast for the first time seemed to expand my heart field beyond the hospital walls, while I groaned with afterpains. I had a "textbook labour" according to Sue, the renowned Hobart obstetrician. Twelve hours of intervention free contractions and a vaginal delivery without a tear. This ideal birthing was what I prepared and longed for. "You have perfect hips for it" reassured Sue. Afterwards I almost felt ashamed to talk about my birthing story with friends who had emergency cesareans. I also haboured guilt for falling pregnant immediately, "You don't muck around!" my partner said.

We had just returned from an expedition to the remote West Coast of Tasmania, perched in tents above jagged rocks hammered by fierce waves. I had been traveling the world as a wilderness photographer. He was teaching architecture. Little did we know just how much our worlds were about to change.

We nestled with little Eider through cold August nights in a haze of love and exhaustion. Our wide-eyed fellow was a poor sleeper, waking every one to two hours and napping inconsistently until his first steps at fourteen months old. His dad and I took turns strapping Eider to our chests to walk the dog or pound the living room floor. As night feeds grew less and milestones passed, I began to wonder whether Eider would be my only child. Wondering turned to knowing: I was not "complete" with one. I longed to do it all again, to give Eider a sibling to play and grow with.

Despite seamless teamwork as parents, on the subject of having multiple children, my partner and I were at a stand still. Before gaining any clarity, I fell pregnant. Another boy! Anxious to finally reach the twelve week mark, we learned that Indi had a chromosomal abnormality incompatible with life. I was shocked and disbelieving. After fourteen weeks gestation, my body felt numb and empty: pregnant one day and not the next, without a baby to show for it. I cried myself to sleep cuddling Eider each night. In the daytime I focused on planning our upcoming wedding. We tied the knot among tall trees before dancing by the outdoor fire while folk tunes whistled into the night. Sadly our honeymoon glow gave way to conflict. My monthly cycles echoed my longing for another pregnancy. Friends offered comfort: "give yourself time to heal". "Maybe later," uttered my husband.

As "later" arrived, I miscarried a second time. This fetus had no heartbeat. I woke after the operation to tears rolling down my cheeks, the nurse patting my shoulder. Grieving was interrupted by multiple trips back to hospital before I laboured at home for nine hours to expel a large blood clot. I had never heard of such a thing. Who had? Women's experiences of miscarriage are rarely discussed, let alone acknowledged by the men in our lives and society at large. We lit candles and received roses and cooked meals as surreal days and nights rolled into weeks. I embodied a volatile cocktail of emotions and hormones, my husband escaping from my furnace to his office. The truth hit hard: we wanted different things. There was no win-win. True heartfelt choices can only be made for ourselves, not for others. I knew what I wanted. So did he. The problem was that we also wanted each other. It was make or break time.

Within months I found myself choosing between a secure life with my husband and son, and a new reality of single motherhood, shared care arrangements and welfare dependency. My father and brother put it bluntly: did I really want to follow in my mum's footprints, as a struggling single parent? I asked for guidance from my Superconscious: Could I overcome my emotions and limiting beliefs in order to parent on my own? What will people say? How would I afford two kids? Would I crumble? The truth was that I was at risk of falling hard. Trauma imprints had tripped me up multiple times. I would need to tender to my trauma responsiveness in order to give birth again, especially alone. I carried enormous fear, guilt and shame around my past with PTSD, especially postnatal PTSD, which was traumatising in itself.

As a new mother, friends commented on how well I was doing, stating that I was "a natural". While mothering felt intuitive it was also very anxiety provoking.

After three weeks of barely any sleep, my world spun and I lost grip on reality, shocking those around me. Over one long night, I spiraled from panic and dissociation to delusion and paranoia. "I can't feel my legs!" I screamed in terror. Each time I drifted close to the sleep I desperately needed, I thought I was dying, which only jerked me awake again. I would not hold my baby to nurse him for the fear of smothering or dropping him. My body convulsed while Eider wailed down the corridors cradled in his father's arms. Riding by ambulance back to hospital, I thought we were driving down the gravel road of my childhood home. At age seven I nearly died in the car mum was driving. My head smashed against the windscreen, shattering the left zygoma bone, leaving my eyeball hanging loose. This early dissociative experience of freezing and dissociating to survive clearly set a switch that reactivated periodically, this time in dramatic fashion.

In A&E, I only grew more hysterical. Flailing around in delusion, I reenacted labour in the hands of warm midwives and perplexed nurses attempting to calm my rapid breathing that on later blood tests would indicate that I was "very unwell". At the greatest point of panic, I saw my baby and me as white lights. I screamed, believing we were both dead, then lay still.

Dad sat by my side, tears streaming down his face. Mum frowned in concern and shook her head before going home for a sliver of sleep. Eider drank formula in a bottle from his scared, wide eyed dad. The frazzled registrar transferred me to the public emergency rooms, where the psychiatrist prescribed a sedative. Finally I slept. In the morning I breastfed my baby and ate breakfast with a smile. I received the only available bed in the private Mother and Baby unit, where despite a few panic episodes, I stabilised after receiving care, medication and help with Eider until we returned home three weeks later. My postpartum experience haunted me as I went about the duties of parenthood. My nervous system seemed irrevocably altered.

Three years on I did not know how to find the courage to birth again. What if it happened again, or something worse? My conscious fear of death and dying was intense, the unconscious patterning clearly a sleeping lion. By this stage tests reported a rapid decline in my fertility. I was stressed and underweight. I missed Eider dreadfully when he was absent, devastated that he was experiencing two separate childhood homes just like I had. My husband and I rode the waves of hurt and anger while sorting legal matters and attempting to co-parent with grace.

I carved out time to heal my inner landscape by attending regular counselling and kinesiology sessions and hiking in nature. I consulted my mentor, Sophie Bashford, whose intuitive gifts and teaching on awakening the Divine Feminine through her Moon Temple membership was pivotal to me finding my power and purpose and to awakening my dormant and often ignored intuitive capacity to receive wisdom from the field. It was frightening to shed lifetimes of neural wiring that it was not safe to be powerfully intuitive. Women have faced centuries of brutal persecution, torture and death for perceived witchcraft and black magic that were actually the sacred feminine arts of midwifery, medicine and knowing beyond knowing. I finally broke through my visceral fear to come out of hiding, learning to consciously create from my intuitive genius, planting the seeds that would become a string of miracles I co-created with the universal field.

I learnt that the first step in intuitive, conscious creation was to choose what I wanted: a healthy baby. This gave my consciousness a future reference point, a desired reality, to focus on.

I then taught all levels of my consciousness that this future was real by regularly having a full sensory experience of it. I felt this baby as if it was in my arms. My heart swelled with love as I imagined it suckling at my breast. I heard sweet cooing and I smelt that new baby smell. Because the mind cannot tell the difference between what is real and what is imagined, my consciousness painted my future as a memory. I then rewired the resistance to having it, neutralizing the fears, worries, doubt, frustration and grief, the beliefs that it may not be possible or that I was not allowed it; and the stories, judgements and inner conflicts that I carried. I intuited each obvious action step towards my end result before taking them: I spoke to potential donors, had tests to be a recipient at the IVF clinic, looked for a place to call home and nurtured my body. I also had to surrender my choice, to be completely fine with how things were in order to create what I wanted. I taught my consciousness that my current reality was not a problem to be fixed and that my future was not better than my present. This is key to intuitive, conscious creation: we must *be it to see it* and we must not regard our current reality or ourselves as broken, otherwise we will create more of what we don't want instead of what we desire.

It was not long until magic manifested as I began to understand that being an intuitive conscious creator is to experience life as a series of miracles and synchronicities that are the result of energetic frequencies in my invisible field matching those in the universal field. The first magic was when, in the midst of a housing crisis, I leased a cottage on the same premises as my mum, next to the soothing sounds of Hobart Rivulet. The gift of moving into such a supported environment increased my optimism that having this baby was possible.

The next miracle appeared as I stayed in *structural tension* with my end result, allowing the energy of least resistance to flow from my current reality towards my true choice. A close friend offered to donate sperm! What an incredible gift: to have a known donor father who had no agenda and who lovingly wanted to help. Although IVF or artificial uterine implantation were options, he agreed on naturally trying to conceive. I intuited, then chose, the end result of conceiving a healthy pregnancy on my birthday weekend and to spend 2021 in a baby bubble. Like a birthday present from the divine, I fell pregnant straight away. Weeks of nausea turned into a week of waiting for this baby to spontaneously initiate labour. Instead, I was to be admitted and induced with gel. Like another gift from the Universe, this was perfect because it caused less anxiety and uncertainty than a trip to hospital in the middle of the night, child in tow.

Birthing my second baby was deeply spiritual. I spent a night of pre-labour listening to solfeggio frequencies and communicating with my spirit guides. While the midwives were dubious and the doula stayed neutral yet devoted, I knew in my bones that my baby was on his way. Sure enough, in less than an hour, he emerged *en caul*: waters intact. Elegantly breaking free of his watery suit, baby G was in my arms within seconds, where he took his first breath of life. Labour was so brief that my male obstetrician missed it. "We women did it!" said one jubilant midwife, thanking me for such a profound experience. Later, when my mum met her fourth grandchild, she excitedly shared that a birth en caul was considered very spiritual across many cultures, occuring in only one in every 80,000 births. I swelled with pride, awe and a beautiful knowing that of course this miracle baby would begin life wrapped in mystique and magic. His buoyant birth gifted him the calmest and least traumatic way to begin life. Named after a prince who became king, Gwydion, "born of trees" was ready to fly.

Now nearly two, Gwydion's presence has always been magnetic. School children squeal in delight while tourists request photos with my golden haired spark. At home he is self-directed and content, and while Eider took some time to adjust, Gwydion's brother soon became his biggest fan and a master protector. A brave knight for the little king.

Unlike my first postpartum experience, this time my care team and I were prepared with low-dose anti-anxiety medication, mum help and a doula on standby. Somehow I got through with relative ease and an enormous pride for doing every night on my own. I was profoundly content. In the months that followed I received support, I got better at asking for it and I found a rhythm of parenting two on my own, relishing the together times and relaxing one-on-one with Gwydion. I even discovered solo-parenting suited my independent spirit, giving me a renewed sense of freedom and empowerment!

I gaze upon my two boys every day with a grateful heart. How lucky am I to be their mum?! Miracles kept coming as I stayed conscious and powerful creating my own life. When Gwydion was four weeks old, I met Rohan, the man who would become my life and business partner and a devoted father for Gwydion.

While starting a new relationship happened earlier than I anticipated, it was again a result of knowing what I wanted and staying in structural tension with that end result while taking obvious intuited action. Together Rohan and I experience co-creation with love, awe, gratitude and joy. We grow and expand through life's challenges and delight in raising these two beautiful boys and creating massive global impact through our work.

In becoming a certified Magnetic Mind Coach, I learnt the language for what I had already been doing as an intuitive creator and took it to the next level, learning how to coach creative structure and a more advanced, rapid rewiring process than what I had used, called the Recode. And, with expert coaching by Chris Duncan, the founder of Magnetic Mind, I rewired my unconscious trauma patterns such that I no longer experience the repetitive illness episodes that plagued me since I was seven. Like the next pearl in a string of miracles, I now teach and coach alongside Chris, helping thousands globally to step into their intuitive, creative genius. This is what it really means to be human: to embody the pure creative spirit we started life out as, just like baby G.

About the Author

Coach and Facilitator at Conscious Education Company; Founder and C.E.O. of the Conscious Creator Collective

Arwen Dyer has a Masters in Creative Arts Therapy, an Honors in Psychology and a Bachelor of Arts, and has spent many years working with trauma survivors. Arwen is a Certified Magnetic Mind Coach and craniosacral therapist. At Conscious Education Company, she facilitates Superconscious Recode sessions and helps teach others how to do the Recode. Privately, Arwen coaches visionary leaders to create big impacts by awakening their intuitive genius. Arwen is an internationally published and awarded nature photographer and budding author. She loves to travel, dance and enjoy nature with her partner and two boys in lutruwita, (Tasmania), Australia.

Email: assist@arwendyer.com
Facebook:
https://www.facebook.com/ArwenDyerIntuitiveCoach
Website: www.arwendyer.com

Lisa Goodhand

In a multicultural world, borders are not where cultures end, but where they begin to share.

Have you ever decided to do something just for fun, with no idea it could change the course of your life? That happened to me when I chose to study Chinese at school – instead of one of the more popular languages – when little was known about China.

Learning Chinese as an Aussie kid has given me a life of adventure, and a career journey that's been an absolute buzz. It opened doors, and opened my eyes to the wonders of cultural differences, and let me travel the globe.

I've been a translator in some unusual – and scary – situations. A federal police officer investigating Asian organised crime. A small business owner helping companies do business in Asia. And I've rarely been in a situation where Chinese hasn't been helpful.

So join me and share my experiences. And along the way, discover some little pieces of wisdom you can apply to your daily life in this multi-cultural universe.

The beginning

It all began in the 1980s, in Darwin, where I decided to learn Chinese in high school. I chose it purely because I liked the intricacy and flow of the written characters. But many people thought there was no future in learning Chinese. Besides, the perceived threat of communism was ever present, especially for older Australians. But I persisted, and fate kept me firmly on this path.

My parents fully supported my choice to learn Chinese. In 1985, when my Chinese teacher in year 10 said we had an opportunity for a school excursion to China, I thought Mum and Dad would never allow it. Instead, they signed me up, packed my bag, and sent me off to the unknown. It was a life-changing experience that opened my eyes to a different world and culture. I was fascinated by everything I saw and heard. The food. The people. The history, and the architecture. I felt a connection with this place that I could not explain.

In 1992, shortly after I started university, I had an opportunity to live and study in China for a year. I told my parents, thinking they would never agree. But shortly after, I packed my bag and headed again to China.

Voice of cultural difference

In the early 1990s, China was a far cry from its modern self, and our university dormitory grounds were basic. Communal showers, no central heating, no television, few cars, millions of bicycles – and chopsticks! As a teenager, I was living in a country where English was alien, the food was unfamiliar, and the surroundings were foreign. It was mentally challenging. I couldn't just pick up a mobile phone or text my friends back home for support every time I was homesick or needed help. I had to build resilience.

Before I left for China, my grandfather sat me down. In his thick Dutch accent, he explained that living in a foreign country without the ability to go home at any time would be hard and mentally challenging. I needed to put blinkers on and not let this get to me. And so persistence became part of my life. My grandfather had survived two years in a prisoner-of-war camp, so I really had no reason to complain.

Despite the challenges, living in pre-modern China was the most exhilarating, character-building and memorable time of my life. Further, the lessons of self-confidence, resilience and persistence have stood the test of time, and they are especially relevant in my business life.

Chinese was my thing

When I could speak Chinese fluently, I realised that this would be permanent in my life. I liked speaking Chinese, I loved the food (probably a bit too much), and I easily moved through the culture. Whether I was sitting on the kerb talking Chinese to a monk, hitchhiking through uncharted townships, or haggling prices in street markets, Chinese was my thing. I instinctively knew it would have a greater purpose in my life, although I still wasn't sure how. I needed to make my own opportunities, as there were no calls for Chinese speakers in the classifieds in those days.

My first job speaking Chinese was in a 5-star hotel in Guangzhou, China. In the early 90s, 5-star was still a relatively new concept. My job as a Westerner was to teach the staff etiquette, and to act as the bridge between the hotel staff and the Western guests. I was also put in charge of the staff choir – a group of Chinese staff who were told they would be in the choir – to sing carols in the lobby during the Christmas period.

There were a few times when I wondered if I could pull this off, but discovered you don't need to be a singer (which I definitely was not) to train someone to sing. You just need to know what the end goal looks like and be able to articulate it.

After my contract ended, I returned to Darwin and became a freelance translator. During those days, there was intrigue with

China, but no solid career paths for Chinese language speakers. So translating it was to be.

Resilience put to the test

One of my most memorable and dangerous translations was on an Australian outback safari with China's CCTV. Supporting a film crew on a documentary series put my Chinese vocabulary to the test. In full camouflage, I stood in waist-high brown water, knee deep in the mud stirred up by buffalo, while I translated a safety briefing. Our guide was telling us what to do if a buffalo attacked. I was petrified, and seriously questioned my decision to be there. But I had a job to do, and somehow got the words out.

It definitely wasn't the best translation I've ever done. Nevertheless, it was the only video of me that appeared on the documentary broadcast in China. While standing in the filthy, crocodile-infested mud, a snake went past. There was only one place for the journalist and me – up the nearest tree!

Chinese translator at AFP

I moved to Sydney, where I decided I could use my Chinese in a real career. I joined the Australian Federal Police, and was fast-tracked through to a specialist group for Asian organised crime. I was the only Caucasian Chinese speaker, and only one of three Chinese speakers in a team of around 20. It became my job to investigate crime syndicates from Hong Kong and China that were complicit in the illegal drug trade.

I thought I'd really found my calling and that learning Chinese was intended for this purpose. The highlight was a massive drug bust during peak hour in Sydney traffic. The Chinese kingpin was getting away from the crime scene by car, to which I was given a very strong command from the senior officer over the radio "DO NOT LET HIM GET AWAY".

I broke land speed records against all odds, pulled the bad guy out of his car, and arrested him in Chinese in front of numerous spectators. At this time, it was one of the largest hauls of heroin and MDMA in Sydney.

But taking millions of dollars worth of drugs off the streets was followed by many weeks in court. When you're one of the only Chinese speakers in your team, criminal barristers take great joy in pulling your translation apart. In any case, resilience won, and the bad guy went to jail.

Voice of small business

I felt it was time to leave the AFP, so I took a leap of faith, and left a secure job to set up my own company. After several iterations, in 2005 I finally established China Blueprint Consultants. The name came from my desire to help Australian companies develop blueprints for their business in China. I aimed to build a bridge between Australian and Chinese companies for better business transactions. In my experience, most bad business transactions resulted from miscommunication or cultural differences. My goal was to fix these.

First, I focussed on import services, and designed my own. I was one of a few consultants providing good communication with research and inspection skills. Others were trying to insert themselves as middlemen, taking massive commissions and absolving themselves of responsibility when quality issues arose.

The beauty of a small business is the ability to be creative and follow your passion, work your own hours, and choose your customers.

But no one tells you about the sleepless nights that come with the worry of where your next dollar is coming from, when problems arise with your customers over expectations. Or when you're not sure if you can make your rent or pay wages. Being a small business owner, at times, can be more exhausting than drug busts and court appearances.

Voice of choosing passion over a mission

Even though I had no formal training in quality inspection or manufacturing processes, my ability to learn quickly, and my willingness to visit hundreds of factories across China with my customers, meant I became a subject matter expert. Understanding both sides' expectations and interpreting them in a way that made sense meant we could limit the problems that arose, or at least attend to them before it was too late.

With time though, and as the trade balance between Australia and China started to even up, I also noticed a definite trend in the market that meant Australia was no longer just importing from China but also exporting. This came with the power of the internet, and global eCommerce was on the rise.

Voice of experience

Again this brought up an opportunity for me to be involved, supporting Australian companies that needed to learn how to go about the process. I was intrigued by eCommerce and the power of the internet. I'd been building my own websites from the beginning, and had a definite flair for marketing.

Why did I change tack? Well, I knew that import consultants like me were becoming an unnecessary expense as the internet took our place. Alibaba was now an importer's direct line to manufacturers, flights to China were cheaper, and generally, the world was becoming more mobile. As a small business owner, you need to be able to read the signs, which sometimes means changing to keep up and avoid disaster.

Phase three of my business, as I would call it, was establishing my business consulting and marketing services to help exporters and brand owners find their niche in China and develop their supply chain, whether online or offline. This included digital marketing services to help them build a brand presence and sales within the Chinese community. Finally, I could sink my teeth into my true love, marketing and design, combined with my other true love, Chinese. It was a match made in heaven.

Since taking on this new direction, I've worked with many wonderful Australian brands. I've developed market entry and marketing strategies for everything from Australian honey to jewellery, olive oil, car wax, skincare, manufacturing equipment, medical devices, dairy products, tourism services, business services, financial services, and more.

There's a saying, 'If opportunity doesn't knock, build a door,' that I live by. For small businesses, this is an essential mindset. Facing the new world in my business, I must tackle the ever-changing environment of new technology, consumer preferences, rules and regulations, and political interference. I built a few doors before I found my true passion, but what matters is the journey that got me here. All those experiences along the way gave me the skills I have today and that guide me through my business transactions.

Voice of new ways to do business

When COVID-19 devastated the business environment and soured the relationship between Australia and China, I had to find new ways to do business. Many marketing budgets bound for China shrank or became non-existent. So once again, I had to find new ways to earn income, as what I offered suddenly had limited appeal. I also had to find ways to deal with the new prejudice against China and my Chinese friends, as people started to point the finger.

I took a new tack and focussed domestically on the local Australian-Chinese market. Despite not having money for international marketing, many brands had to maintain the lines of communication with the massive investments they had committed to Chinese customers. They soon realised that they could market locally to the over 1.5 million Chinese in Australia, using the same Chinese language platforms and technology. This allowed them to maintain communications, and even build their brands, and I was there to support them.

Though occasionally I considered returning to the safety of a public service role, I stuck to my guns, appreciating the beauty of being a small business that enables you to pivot your model overnight.

In my life and career, I have transcended borders and learnt to operate in two very different cultures. Along the way, I've picked up some important life and business skills that have helped me.

Voice of integrity

Translating under the microscope, whether it be criminal barristers in court or under the watchful eye of your customer standing in a factory together, is always challenging. Even when I didn't have all the Chinese words for each of these different scenarios, I had the foundations of language and a commitment to integrity. To admit when I was wrong or when I didn't know something. People can sniff integrity a mile away, and on many occasions, despite my limited technical Chinese, I was quite often called upon as the preferred translator. Whatever you do, always do it with integrity, and you will shine.

Train your team

In small businesses, the cost of staff will be your number one challenge, but it's important to remember that people are your number one asset. In my consulting business, I've had to rely on people unreservedly, when they had conversations with the factories and helped me negotiate the deals. Their Chinese made up for my limitations, and my English made up for theirs.

Language and culture can often shroud problems, so asking many questions and listening to the answers is key to success when doing business in two different languages. Be brave to ask questions when things don't make sense, and remember, culture has a big influence on how people communicate.

Be ready for change

The beauty of being a small business owner is that you can be dynamic and change with relative ease to suit your environment. Don't be scared of what you don't know. Be open to change, and always keep a sharp eye on what's happening over the horizon.

I'll never forget a client who went to China to introduce a car wax product to the market. He thought people in China would clean their own cars, as they do in Australia. However, they didn't, so we changed the plan and targeted the dealerships and detailing stores instead. This open-mindedness to change meant the dream of selling to China remained alive. Just the way it happened was different.

Valuable experiences

Work should be seen as an opportunity to accumulate valuable experiences. I undertook many different roles in my career, but only ones where I could use my Chinese. I worked in a call centre speaking Chinese to Singaporeans. I lived in Hong Kong and translated at a university. I joined the police force and worked for a specialist task force. These experiences came about because I actively pursued them, eventually leading me to my ultimate goal of setting up my own company. My advice is to go out and get as much experience as possible, be it good, bad or indifferent, before starting your small business journey.

During the heyday of my consulting career, I was often required to travel to China. Each time, I would take my daughter, a toddler at the time. Despite her not speaking Chinese and my being busy at work, this did not stop us. I would hire a Chinese-speaking nanny from a qualified agency to entertain her throughout the day.

Before I knew it, my daughter was using Chinese social media apps to communicate with me throughout the day, had learnt how to say "I want ice cream" in Chinese, and had the poor nanny playing hide and seek in a small hotel room for over 4 hours a day.

We also need to have faith in our own ability. I took a client to China to meet with potential buyers for his thermocouple business. With no idea what a thermocouple was, I took on the challenge, learning some new words and a heck of a lot about high-heat manufacturing. The trip was a success. To this day, that client has been in business with Chinese for over 10 years.

Make where you work the best adventure of your life

I enjoyed my work immensely and felt proud of being able to use my skills to bridge gaps and foster understanding between different parties. I also felt grateful for having chosen Chinese as my language of study back in high school. It opened so many doors for me and enriched my life in ways I could not have imagined.

Choosing Chinese was one of my best decisions. Initially, it was not easy or obvious, but it was rewarding and fulfilling. It taught me valuable lessons about myself and the world around me. It also showed me how powerful our decisions can be when we follow our intuition and passion.

I hope this chapter inspires you to make decisions that align with your true self and purpose. You never know what amazing things can happen when you do so. Remember: once you decide, the universe conspires to make it happen.

Lisa Goodhand
Managing Director
China Blueprint Consultants

About the Author

Lisa Goodhand is a top Australian "Trade with China" business consultant. She's also a regular expert contributor to news media, providing fascinating insights and commentary on doing business with China in this digital age. Lisa is one of very few Australians without a Chinese background, who are fluent in Mandarin at a level good enough to do business with China. In an exciting specialist task force for the Australian Federal Police, Lisa investigated Asian organised crime for 4 of her 5 years there.

Her award-winning company, China Blueprint Consultants, has assisted hundreds of satisfied clients extend into the Chinese market.

Lisa loves to travel and is happiest when discovering new places to explore with her two children.

Website: https://www.chinablueprint.com.au
LinkedIn: lisa-goodhand
Facebook: @ChinaBlueprintConsultant

Mary Gouganovski

Unapologetically Me

I always thought it would be a singular event, a moment in time that changes everything. A moment you can't come back from. Maybe I could be sitting somewhere one day, reminiscing and say "yeah, that's the moment my world changed." The catalyst or lynchpin that altered the course of my life forever.

That's not how it happened.

No, looking back, it's been a series of significant blows, some so fast I didn't see them coming; and others, so slow, I didn't see them coming either.

For me, it was a slow growing cancer, a battle I've been fighting in my head since I was old enough to understand my emotions, to know how I was viewed by the world around me.

My body issues have been the underlying cause of so many problems, I never realised quite how badly they pulled me down until recently.

Suffering from Insulin Resistance has left me with a thyroid and metabolism that doesn't work and the company of panic attacks that render me useless in some social settings. My weight has gone up and down, mostly up, since I was a teenager. I could look at a piece of lettuce and put on weight. There's no cure, no easy fix that we know of yet. I had been waiting for so long for something to change, for it to somehow resolve itself. For a way to manage my imbalance of hormones to help me finally lose weight so I can actually live my life or for someone to come along and tell me that I'm pretty enough to exist in this world.

Perhaps that's only in the movies, you know the romantic kind where the gorgeous hunk in metaphorically shining armour comes forward and saves you from yourself? Makes you realise your self worth and empowers you to move forward?

I had been waiting for that for years, putting every part of my life on hold…

It's hard as a woman, especially one who has *Insulin Resistance*, an autoimmune disease that's left me struggling with my weight for as long as I can remember. A *European* woman, in a very Western society, a *young* woman in business… just here trying to keep her head above water in a vast ocean where everything tries so desperately to drag you down.

Before I continue, let me introduce myself. My name is Mary. I have been in business my entire life, it's all I've ever known. For twenty years, I have been immersed in this world. Starting as a humble family business, a little shop in a tiny country town in New South Wales, Australia. Our first Christmas, we were blessed to have customers pouring in, and every day, I'd work the register. I was so small, I couldn't see over the counter.

My anxiety started back then...

"Mumma, how are we going to handle all of these people?" I asked, wide eyed as my

gaze flickered desperately between her loving face and the door. "It's okay baby, you just

stand there and serve them, one customer at a time," she said to me as she put a little stool by the register so I could stand tall enough to see everything I needed to see.

And see, I did...

Let me ask you; Have you ever felt the same? Like you're unworthy? So small and insignificant that nothing you do matters? That you couldn't possibly change yourself, let alone this world? Ever wanted something so badly, felt like it was so close your entire body was vibrating with the need to reach out and take it and yet you always fell short, always missed out?

I did. In a lot of ways, I still do.

I felt like I took up too much space that I didn't deserve, like my silenced voice shouldn't be heard, like my opinion was too loud, too much for the room I was standing in and the people who filled it.

I had been berated and crushed for years on end, the noise around me convincing me that I wasn't enough. I allowed it to chip away at me, piece by piece until I was nothing but an empty shell of the woman I could be. The woman I should be.

There was no singular event, no individual moment that changed my life. It truly was a series of unfortunate events, like life just kept throwing all these curve balls at me. I couldn't possibly keep up, couldn't even voice my pain.

No one wanted to hear it, anyway.

I had spent the last six or seven years like the crab I am, hurt and wounded and hiding under my shell. I couldn't handle any more pain, I couldn't handle any more things breaking me down. In that time, I'd lost our shop, my grandmother, my sense of self, we'd been threatened by the bushfires, by floods all over again, by a pandemic, a war, another financial crisis, the instability around me right now is frightening, the sense of dread and panic in my chest constantly nagging at me until I was too afraid to sneak a glance, to pop my head out in fear of something else hitting me.

Yet as much as I wish I could blame developing my hard, comfortable little shell on those things, it always comes back to my sense of self. To the way I see myself whenever I stand in the cold, harsh light of a mirror. My thoughts run rampant, taking the words of others and using them against myself until there's tears in my eyes and I feel even more unworthy of love, affection, or success.

Even now, as I sit here in my tiny little hotel room in the heart of Gangnam District of Seoul, I've been plagued with intrusive thoughts. Surrounded by so many thin, beautiful people and in a room full of mirrors. I can't seem to escape this torment. The way I convince myself that I don't deserve the opportunity that's been presented to me.

I almost turned it down, walked away from the chance to speak in front of over one hundred people at one of the largest beauty, cosmetic and raw ingredient trade shows in the world out of fear that I don't deserve to take up space just because I take up more than others.

Twelve months ago, I never would have agreed to this, or any of the other opportunities that have come my way in the last year. I was so terrified to be seen, I'd run away from any door that opened… Until one day, I met someone who said, 'Mary, I want to hear what you have to say.' She asked me to tell her my story, and I did. I cried from start to finish, telling her things I'd only ever told my mum before that night.

By the end of it, I'd apologise so many times for everything and nothing all at once. I thought I'd be judged, I thought I'd be told that I wasn't good enough and she was tired of hearing me speak...

Instead, she invited me to tell my story again and again, in my first anthology and on a global stage full of empowering and incredible women.

I couldn't have been more shocked.

I remember getting off that call and immediately starting coming up with excuses as to why I couldn't do it, why this was bad, why no one would want to hear from me. I spent the rest of the night keeping myself awake with all these dark thoughts and disillusions.

Frank Hubert famously wrote, "Fear is the mind-killer. Fear is the little-death that brings total obliteration." For over three decades, that had been my life. It still is to a degree, but he also wrote, "I will face my fear. I will permit it to pass over me and through me. And when it has gone past I will turn the inner eye to see its path. Where the fear has gone there will be nothing. Only I will remain."

While it's easy to say, that sentiment couldn't be more true.

She asked me who I was. I remember the question so clearly, in my mind it was like a freight train that just came to a crashing halt.

I didn't know, I couldn't answer her.

"You've spent so long being Mary Grace," that's the name of my brand, "Is that who you want to be five years from now? Who are you, beyond that?"

I didn't know how to answer her. I was floored with the realisation that I *could be* something more than the business I had built, than the career I'd thrown myself head first into. In all my years, I've never stopped to contemplate who Mary Gouganovski was, who she wanted to be, how to separate her from this all encompassing entity. My mum had been asking the same thing, for months on end she kept saying, "Mary, if you really want things to change, you have to be prepared to let this all go. To walk away." I hadn't understood the depths of her statement until that moment.

It made me realise I had options. Such simple words, such an earth shattering moment for me.

Reminiscing now, I can honestly say, that was the day that *truly* changed my life. It was my singular event, my moment in time, the catalyst that pushed me towards a new path. At that moment, I gave myself permission to exist. I decided that I was going to push past my fear and accept what comes next. My mum was right, she had been all along, I was worthy. I never needed anyone else to tell me what she'd already been saying, what I already knew deep down.

The journey I've been on is nothing short of incredible, though it's far from easy.

We get so used to being the victim, finding comfort in the pain, the devil we know. Using it as a crutch to hold us back, to let the fear win and stop us from finding out what love and hope and joy is really like.

I wish I could tell you it's an overnight success, that I just woke up the next day after deciding to take this leap and everything was perfect, and I never looked back. Whilst it's been the most rewarding year of my life, it's also been amongst the hardest.

Facing thoughts and emotions you'd suppressed for so long makes it all the harder, like ripping a bandaid off a gaping wound, then throwing salt on it. I didn't know at the time just how much parts of my life had affected me.

Sure, it's hard, but when you're in the moment, experiencing it for the first time you're thrown so far into fight or flight, in doing everything you can to survive and escape out the other side with your life, you don't completely comprehend the gravity of the pain you just experienced.

Once you take that first step, it's like pulling the ripcord and watching it all unfold. There's no slow descent, it's a free fall into the abyss of the past.

The first few months were the hardest, I don't think there was a single meeting, phone call or session that didn't end in tears. All because someone outside of my personal lunchbox gave me permission to express myself.

It was like a relentless waterfall.

As I started to tell more of my story and who I was, I started to feel the trauma I'd repressed for so long wrap around me, like a constricting harness that wouldn't relinquish its hold.

I'm someone who feels too much, too sensitive for this world, so I don't process things well at the time they happen. I lost my grandmother four years ago now, and I still haven't been able to look at a single photo of her, or listen to a video I have of her talking to my mum. She was sick for a long time, in a level of pain I couldn't express on paper. Couldn't express it in words.

I still feel like it was just yesterday that I was laying beside her in bed, holding her as we watched reruns of Becker, or listening to her soft, low voice telling me stories of her childhood, of the siblings she hadn't seen in over forty years. She didn't want to die, afraid that her brothers and sisters, or the parents who passed when she was a child wouldn't remember her anymore.

I'm too afraid to live, to look back at her beautiful face and remember what the world was like with her in it. It hurts too much.

Though isn't that the point?

Isn't that what sets us apart?

The fact that we feel so much, means we're still alive. This body I've resented for so long has carried me through every high and every low, has protected me, saved me, supported me. Has taken me through a world of possibilities I never thought possible.

The hits don't stop coming, I'm not sure that they ever do. I've been knocked down harder in the last twelve months than my whole life so far. It's our ability to cope with them that changes. We have a choice, to allow the world to steam roll us into submission, or stand up and fight. To push through to a better tomorrow.

This journey I've been on has shifted my world so dramatically. I've lost friends, gained opinions from others who have been watching me shift and change. Some positive, most negative. When you start to grow and glow, your light shines a little too bright for some.

The most empowering thing I ever did was let myself be open and receptive to looking inward. To learn to bask in my own light, to let it refill my centre and realise that all it does is blast away the darkness and let me live in the now, in the woman I always deserved to be.

My skin is thicker than it ever has been, learning to let others' words and opinions wash off me like water off a duck's back. There'll always be a carrot dangled in front of you, trying to veer you off the path you're on, but it's up to you to keep going. To keep pushing through, day by day, little by little it gets easier to handle. Until you become a pro at knowing how to handle any hurdle, any obstacle on your own. Knowing precisely how to lift yourself up, support yourself, praise you above all others.

Become your own armour.

Sometimes all it takes is that one person giving you permission, it doesn't matter what that is. Telling you that your existence matters. That you alone can make a change to this world.

It came to me at the most unexpected time, I wasn't ready for it, you never will be.

The one constant in life is that there is no constant. I can't always promise a life of sunshine and roses but they'll always surround you, always be there to lift you up. There's no perfect time to change your world, but when it starts, it'll always be the right time.

Talk a walk through the forest of your pain, feel every tree and branch and wildflower, then keep walking. What's waiting for you on the other side is better than you could ever have imagined.

Here in this tiny little hotel, I give you the permission to feel, to live, to tell your story. Whether you write it down, sing it out, tell a friend, tell me, a higher power - it doesn't matter. There's no structure, no rules, no required way to start. The most important thing is that you do. Even if that first step is your name on a piece of paper, sometimes writing just that is more powerful than anything else you could do.

Recognize who you are, who you want to be, all that you need is already within, I promise you.

Once you get a taste of empowerment, you won't get enough.

The free fall now isn't into the dark abyss of your trauma, it's into the open sky of your new life. A life full of stars to guide your way, of clouds to catch you when you stumble, of gentle rain to wash away your pain, the warmth of the sun on your face reminding you of love and joy.

Tell your story, don't hold back.

I'll be waiting for you on the other side, my darling. I cannot wait to see who you become.

About the Author

Mary Gouganovski is the founder of Mary Grace, an award-winning Australian beauty and lifestyle brand specialising in natural, sustainable, ethical, and cruelty-free formulations for the face, body, and home. Starting out in the family's beloved small-town candle boutique over twenty years ago, Mary developed a work ethic at a young age and found passion in the day-to-day challenges and triumphs of entrepreneurship.

She holds a Bachelor in Business and Commerce Majoring in Marketing, a Certificate 4 in Small Business Management and a Diploma in Copywriting. Currently residing in the southern highlands of NSW, Mary is a self-taught entrepreneur, community advocate, and budding motivational voice.

In her spare time, she enjoys books and movies, and functions on coffee and adrenaline.

Instagram: @marygouganovski
Website: www.marygouganovski.com
Linktree: https://linktr.ee/marygouganovski

Nicole Grelecki

Slay the dragon of fear

Do you have scars? Every scar has a story.

Lord knows I have scars like the one on my shin in the shape of California that tells stories of sliding into bases, or the constellation of surgical scars on my arms that tells the story of when I was injured at work. The largest scar isn't one anyone can see. It wasn't caused by any one accident or injury.

This invisible scar was caused by a hard layering of many things throughout my life, like a hard scab on your knee that gets bigger each time it breaks open. Eventually, this festering wound started wreaking havoc on my health. It could no longer be ignored. Something had to be done.

Now, the scar serves as a reminder of my resilience and growth. It is a reminder of how I "slayed the dragon of fear," and transformed into the woman I am today.

In 2005, I thought I had it all figured out. I was a college graduate, working as a police officer, attending law school and planned to work for the US Federal Bureau of Investigations ("FBI"). I knew my path. Nothing could stop me.

Then, in 2007 a career-ending injury changed everything. I was permanently disabled as a police officer, not going to law school, not headed for the FBI and even though marriage scared me, I followed my heart down a new path and got 'hitched' anyway. In due time, we were blessed with two amazing daughters.

In 2019, I was in my 40's and I wanted to be the BEST wife and mother, but also wanted more for myself. I found myself wrestling with internal conflict. I wondered, "was there room for both?" And, then shame set in and I thought, "I didn't deserve both. I should be happy with a loving husband and two strong healthy girls." But I wasn't.

And then, The COVID Pandemic of 2020 happened. The whole world shut down. Everyone was stuck at home and the future was uncertain. There was global fear, many in the US were fighting, and some, like myself, started to reflect on their purpose in life.

"Is this it?" I remember asking myself, "Am I really proud of the person I am? Do I even know who I am?" I didn't know the answers but I knew ONE thing... I wanted something different.

I knew my family was relying on me and yet, I didn't know how to access the joy or energy I was seeing in others. I was tired of wearing the hard shell of armor I had layered on over the years to keep the bad out. I felt weighed down with a thousand pounds of armor in a pile of quicksand, stressed and I was tired. What I realize now, is that my armor wasn't just keeping the bad out, it was also not letting the good in.

The turning point came when I started looking for some guidance as a new business owner. I wanted to create something different, but wasn't sure what. I came across an advertisement for a program by Dean Graziosi & Tony Robbins. It was through this program that my "self-development" and "growth mindset" were born. It was the beginning of manifesting more of the things I wanted and less of the things I didn't, like fear. The first step was facing that fear. No one could have anticipated the can of worms I was about to open.

My first recollection of character-altering fear was when my parents started their divorce. I was eight and we had just moved from the southside to the northside of Chicago. In hindsight, that moment felt very much like the COVID Pandemic decades later; the health and future of my family felt uncertain and everyone was fighting.

I was painfully shy as the youngest of four girls. There were many years where I felt like I was stuck in the vortex of a chaotic tornado, swirling around with fighting and manipulation all around me. Everyone wanted me to be on their side and yet, neither side felt like a safe choice. It was the beginning of feeling the stress in my head, neck and back.

It was hard to know: who I could trust, how I was supposed to act, or who I was supposed to be. I just wanted to feel safe and loved. My identity was something I thought about a lot, often acquiescing to the label of a "tom boy" so people would stop asking me so many questions about why I dressed and acted a certain way.

I never felt like it was something I could discuss, especially because I felt like my Dad's second wife was fixated on making me more "girly."

My sisters were busy with their own lives and my parents were trying to redefine theirs. I decided I was going to do the best I could to stay out of trouble and not worry about what other people thought about me. I was just going to be me!

During the divorce, I was put in court ordered therapy for a short time and it was a disaster. I didn't gain any useful coping or life skills. Instead, in my adolescent mind, I was scared that it was ME that was the problem. If it was me, I didn't want anyone to know.

Everything around me felt scary: new school, new friends, new community, and then the dynamic of my family disintegrating.

My Dad was forced to leave, my mom went to work, my sisters moved out, and I often felt "left behind" with everything out-of-my-control. And although older siblings moving out is a natural progression of a family, I was feeling like it was my fault, suffering in silence and feeling alone.

I quickly figured out I could either keep feeling paralyzed with fear and end up truly alone OR not let the fear stop me from doing the things I longed to do. I had to figure out how to take control.

Taking control as an 8-year-old looked like asking for help from trusted adults like teachers, coaches, and neighbors. And then, as I grew older, it looked like pushing myself to be the best in everything I did and taking leadership roles. Gradually, I made friends, networked with my community by babysitting, and started to excel.

In hindsight, I realize that as I got more involved and developed more life skills my confidence improved. The most important skill I learned was how to be RESILIENT. How to persevere despite the discomfort and try again. When someone told me it was "impossible," I found "I'm Possible".

But there was a flaw in my reasoning as I got older. I was very good at getting up, but I hadn't learned that mistakes were necessary for success.

So with each mistake, the feeling there was something wrong with me was further enhanced. If something was wrong with me, people would leave, and then I would be alone. With every mistake, the fear of unworthiness became a hardened shell, which started to take the shape of a dragon I carried on my back.

The "chaos tornado" of my parents divorce was still swirling when I was in high school. As the youngest daughter, I felt like I was tumbling through the chaos all alone. I was working hard and achieving academic and athletic success, but I had no one to relate to at home and personal issues that felt too big to share with friends.

High school sports and my peers were my world. They met my desperate teenage need for a sense of belonging. But, I was hiding a dark secret. As a way to "get control" in my life I stopped eating. It felt like the only thing I could establish control over. I remember thinking, "if I was the perfect size and shape, then maybe I would feel loved and not alone?" This is absolutely ridiculous when I think about it now, but at the time, I was so scared of ending up alone. The fear of not belonging had taken over.

When I was a sophomore in high school my basketball coach, whom I loved, told me I couldn't play until I got my health in order. My lack of eating had gotten out of control. At first, I was shocked, then annoyed… at myself. My secret was exposed!

I felt like I was failing everyone: myself, my parents, my coaches, my teammates and even my sisters and their kids. With all the responsibility I had taken on as a high-achiever, the disappointment left me feeling overwhelmed and even more alone. It had to be ME, I was anorexic. What had I done?

Sometimes, it's not about what tweens and teens are saying, but what they ARE NOT saying that could do the real damage. It took me several weeks to get my health back in order. With the help of my trusted coach, I was able to rejoin my basketball team on the court.

I was good at getting back up, but once again, I added another thick layer of armor as a way of self punishment. I had no idea what to do or how to fix it.

I fed the dragon a helping of shame and the weight I was carrying got heavier.

I may have been playing basketball again, but I did what any teenager would do who feels lost and hopeless. I started engaging in risky behavior. I moved out of my mom's house when I was 16. I tried to live with my Dad and his second wife, but that was a toxic environment and it forced me to look elsewhere for shelter and love. I ended up at my sister's, with her husband and two small kiddos.

The distance I drove to school came with lots of responsibility and even more independence. I had mastered how to get away with as much as I could and still fulfill my responsibilities. I excelled in high school, worked several jobs, and played sports every season of the year. And yet, I still found time for drinking, smoking, and sneaking out.

And then it happened... I found myself in the wrong place, at the wrong time, with the wrong people, totally intoxicated. What happened was unspeakable. I couldn't tell anyone. I even lied to the police when they called. I felt the weight of the world crash down and sink me further into my self-destructive behaviors. I certainly didn't love myself and I remember thinking, "NO ONE could ever love me."

I carried these hardened layers of shame, unworthiness and fear for years. Always scared that someone would eventually see the weight of these things in the shape of the dragon I carried. It felt inevitable that they would eventually leave or realize I wasn't worthy of the love they had for me. This included my own family.

And then, as I sat in a business training session with Dean Graziosi in 2020, he encouraged us to stop running. I was part of a big group, but I felt like he was talking directly to me. It was time to stop trying to outrun, outwit, or hide the dragon I was carrying called fear. He encouraged me to face my dragon, and let it go! It was exactly what I needed, at exactly the right time. I slayed the dragon of fear and I was free!

I was shocked! I was in disbelief. Could it be as easy as a choice? I felt a sensation deep inside me. Was it fear? This feeling was different. It was light, cool, and hopeful. Then, I realized… it was forgiveness.

The storm had passed and I was free from the weight of the dragon. I chose to release myself from all the old negative stories I had retold myself for years. And although it took a lot of work and a big investment in myself, the festering wound this fear dragon had caused, began to heal.

Without those old stories, hope was possible. I was exactly who I needed to be. Everything in my life was happening for me. I started to feel empowered to find the gift of everything. I felt a fullness in my heart beginning to overflow. I finally believed I was capable of happiness, joy and overflowing energy.

As the healing continued, I was able to give the gift of forgiveness to: myself, my parents, my family, and even the people with unspeakable actions. Then after forgiveness, came love. Self love, love for others, and love for others loving me.

It was like closing the can of worms once and for all and then opening the floodgates of empowered action. I started by reflecting on my expertise and experience as a police officer &

teaching in the schools. I started serving and helping others. I reached out to new and old contacts and began to take action on my new sense of purpose and developing a company fully aligned with my values.

I am so grateful for that pivotal moment in 2020 when I slayed my 40 year old dragon of fear and my growth mindset was born. Over the last 4 years, guided by coaches, mentors and peers I have successfully transformed my dragon of fear into stories of resilience and growth. My fear is simply feedback that is meant to be honored and embraced.

Trusting my fear and treating it with kindness and curiosity, versus anger and resentment, has allowed me to embrace my vulnerability, follow my passions, and take courageous action both personally and professionally. I am finally able to feel the happiness and joy in the success I feel every day, being a better version of myself today, than I was yesterday.

My success includes improving my self-awareness, emotional intelligence, and self-discipline. Continuing to develop and nurture these qualities has empowered me to overcome obstacles, cultivate resilience, and lead a more fulfilling and meaningful life. Now, I harness my fear and use it to fuel my courage to navigate life's adversities and to help others with theirs.

One of the first things I did was to give my first gift of forgiveness to my parents, and especially my mom. I want her to know how much I appreciate: her strength and courage to allow me to shine my own light and how much I love that she is a part of my family's life as we continue to navigate our relationship. Mom, "I do not live my life in spite of you, I have a life, because of you."

Then, I was able to have a positive impact under my own roof with my oldest daughter. I had recognized how fear was starting to paralyze her as she entered her preteen years. She didn't want to move up levels in ice skating or try anything new or different. Everything became scary.

I shared my new belief that fear is part of humanity and that mistakes are necessary. Without fear and mistakes we are unable to achieve our next level of success. Therefore, lean into fear and welcome mistakes. There's only one simple thing to do when you fall, get back up! Now, she uses the tools and strategies I have taught her to help her overcome these moments of paralysis.

She has transformed into a fierce, fearless, gentle flower. In fall 2022, she surprised all of us with a solo in one of her Stage School performances. I was a speechless, teary-eyed, proud happy Momma in the stands that day. She had done it. #togetherwearestronger

I feel honored to continue to assist one of my sisters, through her own swirling tornado of a divorce. She often calls me for guidance and grounding. We focus on love, empathy and compassion. I have helped her improve her emotional well-being, which has improved her communication with her two teenage sons. She also feels more resourceful as she continues to navigate her new situation. And together, we continue to surf the waves of grief after the death of our Dad in June 2021.

As a Certified Teen Coach, I have helped one of my clients improve their emotional well-being, increasing her quality of life score of "school" from 3 to 9. In addition, they have felt a reduction in their anxiety and stress resulting in an improved quality of sleep in less than 12 weeks.

Everyone has their own life's adversities, but these life adversities do NOT determine their infinite potential! Life is only happening for you. All your fears are not roadblocks meant to impede your forward progress. Fears are gifts sent to us from within. If you allow them, they can serve as the feedback you need in order to discover your life's infinite potential.

I chose to be a teen coach, because I don't want tweenagers, aged 10-15, and their families to let fear start to paralyze them during their transformative years and carry the burden of shame and unworthiness for as long as I did. There is a lifeline of hope available and I will continue to cast it to whomever needs it.

I am proud of the wife, mother, sister, and daughter I have grown to be.

Just as I did as a police officer, I choose to use my fear as fuel and run towards the chaos that overwhelms others and help them to the other side. As a coach, I am the teen's (and family's) partner, mentor and cheerleader. I help them to love and trust themselves enough to let their unique gifts be seen.

Now it's up to you! Will you let fear continue to paralyze your family? Or do you want to slay the dragon of fear and learn to transform it into the fuel that moves you forward? It is one simple choice… what will you choose for your family?

About the Author

Nicole Grelecki is a wife to a loving husband, mother to two awe-inspiring daughters, and an Entrepreneur. She is living a life by her design, building her dream home and grateful for every day she has with her 16 year old Maltese, Zeena (the Warrior Princess.)

The former Police Officer has transformed her old disempowering stories of fear into stories of resilience and growth. She helps tweenagers, aged 10-15, (and their families) transform their fears, improve their confidence, and start taking action towards becoming leaders in their own lives.

Facebook, Instagram, Tiktok: @nicolegrelecki
Free Facebook Community: Inspire Tweenager Life Skills

Alana Mills

"Get up! Straighten your crown and become all you were destined to be!"

Who am I

From my earliest memories I have felt like an alien from another planet. I have always felt 'out of place' in a very confusing world ~ often being described as a deep thinker, with an intense personality.

Growing up in the 1970's on a semi remote cattle property in central Queensland, meant contact with the outside world was somewhat limited as I was home schooled until the age of 10 with only my older brother as a playmate.

As such I loved to read and in the 1970's we had a record player and I would love to listen to the story via long playing record and follow along in the book. One of my favourite fairytales was that of Cinderella. I recall even before being able to read I would carefully take the little record out of it's pocket at the back of the book and listen intently to the story. I knew it off by heart but for some reason it spoke to me in a deeper way than just a sad story with a happy ending.

You know it don't you? The poor young woman who was treated so horrendously by her evil stepmother and stepsisters for so many years. Enter her magical fairy godmother and animal friends (mice) who provide her solace and some sanity. They send her off to the grand ball to win the heart of her prince. I guess the rest is history! She lives happily ever after.

She finally becomes what she was destined to be all along, she found who she was and where she fitted! There was hope for me after all! All I had to do was grow up and things would suddenly fall into place. I would discover who I really was and where I fitted in this crazy confusing world.

Where do I fit

By age 9, it had become all too much for my mother to home school, help work the property, do household chores and manage the bookwork that accompanied the running of a one hundred-thousand-acre property.

So, I stepped inside a school gate for the first time in 1980 and was enrolled in a fifth-grade class.

I was an eager learner and was immediately promoted to the advanced mathematics and english class(grade 6/7 level). My true passion was ancient history though. I had become enamoured, almost obsessed with ancient Egypt and in particular, archaeology. In my spare time on the property, I would go for walks down the paddock to see if I could find any old bones. I think it was a bit frowned upon by my parents to have a bone collection, so a rock collection was the next best thing.

I surmised that archaeology would provide me with the information I so deeply sought in my adolescent mind. Ancient Egypt had been described as the dawn of civilization and it must hold the clues to why I was here and to my destiny! To this end I was determined to become an archaeologist.

As I grew into a teenager, I became increasingly more confused with my identity as most teenagers are. This was worsened by the fact my associates (teachers, classmates) questioned my family bloodline. I was constantly asked if I was Greek, Italian, Maltese, Lebanese or Spanish. This might not seem significant but to a 13-year-old girl who by all accounts looked very little like her immediate family became an issue to me. I became more confused as to who I really was and where I fitted.

As my teenage years sped past my dreams of becoming an archaeologist quietly faded as weekends were always spent working on the property as there was always plenty to do. I knew this wasn't where I belonged though and at the age of 17, I went off to college to study a two-year Diploma in Business ~ a safe bet that would be assured to land me a job. I graduated in 1989 and started working in the hotel/resort industry. In the early 90's this was a booming industry in Australia. After moving around Queensland working in the hospitality/tourism sectors I finally made my way home to launch my own business.

I had studied beauty therapy whilst working and had earned another Diploma. After a 3 relationship that had recently failed, I threw myself into my business. It was 1992, Emerald was booming due to the influx of families taking jobs in the mines.

I was only 21 at the time and had the rest of my life ahead of me. Perhaps having a business would provide me with the inner peace and contentment I had been craving. Perhaps this was my destiny!

My business quickly grew and before I knew it, I moved to larger premises and had 4 part-time employees. I still wasn't happy! Why?

I should be happy, shouldn't I? I was making a good living, working super long hours and building a good business reputation yet on the inside I felt empty and worthless.

My fairytale crown...not to be

At age 27 I got married. It was time to settle down. Between us (my ex-husband and I) we purchased two properties, one a house in town and another on some acreage just out of town. It was lovely. On the weekends I worked hard in the garden, and we had some chickens and ducks. We would waterski with friends in the summer months and my business was very successful. Yet, I felt huge waves of guilt, I still wasn't fulfilled.

For our first wedding anniversary we toured Egypt. I recall standing on the Giza plateau overlooking the pyramids, imagining what life would have been like when the gold capstone adorned the top of the great pyramid. If the answers to any of my questions about the origins of human civilization existed here, they departed long ago with the pharaohs that once ruled this once opulent kingdom.

Upon returning home I once again threw into my business. At that time one of my employees was attending The Salvation Army church. She invited us along and instantly I knew this was where I belonged! To cut a long story short, in 2002 I sold my business and my ex-husband, and I moved to Sydney to study fulltime for 2 years to become Salvation Army Officers, (full-time ordained ministers).

I loved the study, the social life and all that Sydney had to offer. We made some good friends, and it wasn't all study and work.

There was plenty of good times making the most of the Sydney beaches and sights.

After graduating in December 2003, we were posted to a small town in the northern New England region of New South Wales. After spending 5 years there serving the community and two children later, our 'marching orders' came from our leaders(bosses) to move. During this time my father had passed away after a battle with dementia, I was suffering post-natal depression (kept very private) with a toddler and a baby and was attempting to work almost full time. It was hard but I was made of tough stuff with a good dose of pride and stoicism thrown in. And so here I was packing up again, this time to move slightly north to south Queensland.

This posting was busy, or I was busy! I suffered a miscarriage in the first year there. My bub's heart just stopped beating and so I had a D and C (dilation and curette) to remove the fetus. I will always remember the feeling of utter emptiness that engulfed me as I woke from the anaesthetic. It was then I came to fully understand the depths of what women endure having a termination to a pregnancy (despite the circumstances).

People tried to be helpful in the days and weeks to come but I really didn't want to discuss it. I was angry! Angry with God! I even remember someone saying, "All you needed was more faith and perhaps you wouldn't have lost the baby". That was exactly what I DIDN'T want to hear! And by the way, is totally untrue and makes no sense!

Another beautiful daughter came along in 2011. Now with three children under 5 and an ever-increasing workload I was becoming tired, very tired. And so, in 2013 we were told we were moving again. Back to New South Wales. Packing, cleaning and writing a 'brief' (the name is extremely bogus, it's a 27-page document from memory) for our replacements (the Salvo Officers that followed us) I was feeling overwhelmed, but the show must go on (so to speak).

It was here in this appointment (placement) that my marriage started to fall apart. The stress in this appointment was even greater as we were overseeing the welfare and spiritual needs of not one, but two country towns. I was becoming tired and jaded with my work as we were constantly under resourced for the needs that were to be met.

I remember one occasion when a young woman walked into our welfare office. She looked like someone had squeezed almost every last inch of life out of her. I asked her to sit down and enquired how I could help. She spoke in an almost robotic fashion, "I was wondering if you could help me, my baby died a couple of days ago and I have no money to bury him." My heart broke and tears still well up today as I write these words. That instance will stay in my mind forever. I had little resources, but I did what I could that day to help her.

The stress took its toll on my marriage and with my history of failed relationships it seemed sadly this was to be no different. This wasn't to be my Cinderella story, my fairytale happy ending and we officially separated in January 2018.

Get up, straighten your crown and become all you were destined to be

It was at this time, I also resigned as an Salvation Army Officer. I was tired and jaded, totally perplexed by some things that occurred during my career and needed to step away to try and reconcile my thoughts and feelings.

Fortunately, I had also studied health and fitness during my time as an Officer and I had that to fall back on to earn a living. As the months went on my life began to slowly unravel. If there was ever such a thing as a 'nice divorce', mine wasn't. To make matters worse, at age 49 my body went into full blown menopause.

I questioned myself in every way, as a woman and as a mother as shared custody arrangements of the children became increasingly complicated. There were arguments with unkind words said on both sides. I said and did things towards my ex-husband which I am not proud of and never will be. Such is the nature of divorce.

Then the recording started in my mind ~ you're not good

enough, not even as a mother. I even contemplated something I hadn't thought of since I was a teenager. Maybe everyone would be better off... (I will let you fill in the rest).

Then one night, it was towards the early hours of the morning, I was dreaming. In my dream, I saw this broken woman, she had long thick hair tied up in a bun with streaks of mascara running down her tear-stained face. Where her hair bun was once neat and pulled tightly up on top of her head, was now messy and straggly. I looked and she had a beautiful crystal tiara atop her head, but it was so crooked I feared it would fall and shatter into tiny pieces. She was sobbing and with every sob, the sight of her became more and more bedraggled. The sight of her was so desperate, she seemed so alone and so hopeless. In my dream I called out to her, but she couldn't hear me! Why couldn't she hear me? I just wanted to help her!

Then a voice came, loud and clear to pierce the sound of the sobbing. It wasn't my voice, it was from somewhere else. "Get up and straighten your crown and become all you were destined to be"! I woke up with a jolt, yet the voice was still there my mind repeating those words ~" Get up, straighten your crown and become all you were destined to be."

I knew that voice, it had spoken to me in the early hours of the morning before, but I thought it had left me. It was God's voice, and I was that woman in the dream/vision, whatever it had been. So even though I felt worthless, God did still love me, He hadn't left me as I had so sadly felt.

From that time on I decided to seek help and in doing so I found out something about myself that now in hindsight makes perfect sense. It seems I have lived most of my life with ADHD (attention deficit hyperactivity disorder). Finally, I had the answers I had sought all my life, such as feeling like an alien on a weird confusing planet. In addition, many people with ADHD don't do relationships well. So many things finally made sense to me now.

I went back to studying and gained certification as a Wellness/Health Coach and eagerly started working with women to empower them to be all they were destined to be.

I have given you a voice

However, my challenges were far from over and I was still fighting a five-year legal battle with my ex-husband. Again, I was becoming weary and emotionally battered from the fight and was about to throw in the towel. I had the support of some good friends who encouraged me to preserve and then the same voice came to me again. "I have given you a voice, you have a voice now, you must speak up for yourself." I immediately thought, 'I am going to do this, not only for myself and my daughters but for the multitude of women that never got the opportunity to speak in a court of law.'

The final court hearing day arrived, and I knew I was going to be cross examined by my ex-husband's barrister. Something I never ever imagined I would have to do. I remembered the words that had been given to me weeks prior ~ I have given you a voice! Even though I was nervous I placed my right hand on the bible that had been brought to me and said these words ~ 'I would tell the truth, the whole truth and nothing but the truth so help me God. 'And He certainly did help me that day. I won my case in court!

Fast forward to the present day, I still have challenges in my life, (who doesn't right) however the way I view and approach these challenges is completely different to the woman I was several years ago.

I have learnt to let go of a lot of anger. I don't blame anyone for things of the past. It is just that, the past and it has shaped me to be the strong woman I am today, for that I am thankful.

There is so much to look forward to in this next chapter of my life. I am amazingly blessed by those around me who love me unconditionally and I am incredibly blessed to be doing what I believe is my purpose for being dropped on this crazy planet (lol).

What is it, you ask? My purpose, my calling is to empower women to become all they were destined to be! I have women come to me, exhausted, confused, having lost their sense of purpose and meaning in life. They come to me with a metaphorically 'crooked crown'. My purpose is to journey with them, to impart to them the tools, the knowledge ~ to bring out the power they possess deep within to straighten their crown! To be 'women of purpose' who work with their innate strengths, who know their true value in life and ultimately be a 'Voice of Power'! A powerful voice in a world that so desperately needs more women to speak their truth, their story ~ a story that has the power to bring connection, purpose and healing to those that hear it!

Blessings friends,

Perhaps we will meet one day!

About the Author

Alana is an Accredited Wellness Coach, a Nutrition coach and Fitness professional. With over 20 years' experience in the wellness and fitness sectors she cites her greatest achievement as mother of 3 beautiful daughters. She loves blogging, reading and running! She lives in Brisbane, Queensland, Australia.

With major life changes including a divorce, navigating menopause and recently being diagnosed with ADHD she has finally found her purpose ~ to empower women over 40 to 'flourish' in this season of their life.

She works with women's innate strengths as pathways to happiness to achieve success in their wellness goals. Providing the right amount of coaching, support and accountability enables her clients to become the best version of themselves.

Email: alana.mills@voiceofpower.com.au
Website: https://voiceofpower.com.au
LinkedIn: https://www.linkedin.com/in/alana-mills-04a23b219/

Kitty O'Brien

Where are you going to be in five years from now?

Are you going to be living more of "the same", or do you see yourself living the dream?

I found myself asking the same question several years ago. I was pacing around my bedroom, desperately worried about the future, until I realised the future isn't made tomorrow. It's made today.

Our stories do not start when we are born. They begin when we are carried in the womb. So I can safely say I did not end up where I did overnight. One year, something significant happened, and it all started with a photo my Mother had taken. The image was of me, and it shook me to my core. I would love to share my whole story with you, but for legal reasons, I can't. Maybe someday I will be able to, as I know I'm not alone in what I've been through. For now, here is the story I can share.

My Mum was trying to capture a happy moment, but in reality, it was heartbreaking. Looking at the photo, I could feel something physically move inside my head. I can't quite explain the feeling. I was shocked, stunned, and in disbelief. My eyes couldn't, not see what I was seeing. I looked like I was dying. My hair was thin and falling out, the glands on my neck were swollen, my eyes were bloodshot, and acne covered my skin. I was pale and frail looking. I didn't recognise myself. I looked at my face every morning in the mirror, but it occurred to me that I had stopped seeing myself a long time ago. The Mayans believed a camera could capture part of your Soul in a photo. This photo showed me that my Soul was broken. That photo made me understand, like never before, that I lived in Domestic Abuse and Coercive Control.

At that moment of rock bottom, I asked myself where I would be in five years. I decided to make a pact with the Universe that I would be free, safe and happy. I promised myself I would be living my best life. And so I planned my escape.

Fast forward the clock, and I am in a very different place. I feel happy, powerful and fully alive.

> *"All men dream; but not equally. Those who dream by night in the dusty recesses of their minds Awake to find that it was vanity; But the dreamers of day are dangerous men. That they may act their dreams with open eyes to make it possible."* - T. E. Lawrence

I am a very different person than that broken Soul in the photo. It has taken years of personal development, but I can now see exactly how I got there. If I had to describe my past self, I had limiting self-beliefs, was trauma bonded to my perpetrator, had extreme anxiety, showed symptoms of Post Traumatic Stress Disorder, lacked confidence and self-love, and had non-existent personal boundaries. In addition, I was in constant fight-and-flight mode; I had hair loss and memory loss, my body was failing, and I had mountains of debt.

I decided to return to University and study Counselling to receive my qualification. Then I studied Quantum Physics as a hobby, which led me to explore the Kybalion Universal Law, the powers of the Subconscious Mind and Dream Analysis. The book "The Magic" by Rhonda Byrne put everything I learned into practice. I discovered a whole new me when I combined this with my Child Development qualifications. I developed powerful coping techniques to help me stay resilient. I recognised how trauma is stored in our nervous system and needs to be released. My biggest lesson was learning forgiveness, self-love and nurturing my inner child.

I developed exercises to help me discover the core of who I am. I reshaped my paradigm, which in turn reshaped my world. I also learnt how to obtain greater happiness, health and love by understanding my behaviour and removing negative blocks.

Hand over heart, I have never had it so good, and I know the best is yet to come!

My story is for women who have hit rock bottom, feel "stuck", tired of their current situation, or for women who know there is more to their life than "this". We shape and colour ourselves and our world with our thoughts and feelings. If you could paint your dream, what would you paint, and what colours would you use?

> "If we can see it in our minds, we can hold it in our hands". - Bob Proctor

If we can imagine it, we are capable of having it. Through our inner world, we can live in an environment that brings us happiness, health and wealth. I am genuinely honoured that I can help people achieve this using my personal experience and my qualifications.

Here are a couple of clients I've helped, Krystal and Susie.

Krystal came to me by contacting me on Facebook. She had been watching my story unfold for a while and decided she was ready to change her life. She was also a survivor of Domestic Abuse and Coercive control and had already begun some of the inner work needed. Krystal had completed the short free course "Living with the Dominator" run by The Freedom Programme and was now ready to live her life to the fullest.

I worked with Krystal one-to-one for three months, and she even decided to join me in business afterwards! Krystal came to me with limiting beliefs that had been deeply conditioned into her. She would self-sabotage the minute positive opportunities came her way. Krystal told me she felt like she had no personal boundaries and would often commit to things she didn't want to, and some people would make her feel small and childlike. Krystal lacked confidence and self-esteem, which in turn, affected her motivation and drive. Krystal focused on everything she disliked about her life and often played the "worst-case scenario game". At times she felt her life was a constant struggle with debt mounting up and never having time for herself. Krystal worked hard at her jobs, but no matter how much she earned, her bank account was empty at the end of each month. She had decided enough was enough and wanted change.

When I work with anyone, I teach them how the brain works as a starting point. We look at the conscious and subconscious mind and how to find a balance between the mind and the body. I ask my clients to write out their timelines, and we briefly examine the attachment theory. This first step is significant because how can we make lasting changes if we don't understand how we are wired?

Krystal could pinpoint the exact moments where limiting beliefs originated in her timeline. This exercise helped her unpack and delve deeper. She could instantly see where her belief system came from using her new knowledge of how the brain functions. She shifted from powerless to empowered, and Krystal started making informed choices and was consciously aware of her thought patterns.

From there, Krystal learnt about the Universal Laws and how these work with what is happening internally and in our external environment. What you are feeling, and thinking is what you attract into your life. What are you attracting in your life?

There are some prominent theories and concepts in this part of the teaching. Most of my students found this section more challenging because they believe life is happening to them and not for them. When Krystal started to understand and embrace the Laws that govern us and our world, she began to get really clear on what she wanted from life. Krystal started to step into her power.

Our confidence grows and blooms when we start stepping into our personal power. I taught Krystal that our emotions and thought patterns have unlimited power in creating our reality. We have more than six thousand thoughts daily, so we must feel our way through the day. We can feel good through the positive emotions of gratitude, forgiveness, desire, faith, love, sex, romance, enthusiasm, courage and hope. The negative emotions are anxiety, depression, fear, jealousy, hatred, greed, revenge, superstition and anger. Krystal found this particularly difficult as she was so used to being negative, and she would find it challenging to be positive for a period of time. Through meditation and journalling, I helped her to break this mindset. Krystal was determined to have a breakthrough, and she did! When we understand our emotions and mindset, we can master them.

Money can be easy to earn if you believe that to be true. You don't have to "work hard" when you work from a place of abundance. Krystal worked from a place of fear and not having enough. She came from a place of lack and low self-worth. Krystal lived and breathed scarcity and worried about mounting debts and just scraping by. Money is not the entirety of wealth, but it makes up a portion of it. Wealth comes from within, and as Bob Proctor said, "We were born rich". I helped Krystal break down some of her money blocks, and she now benefits from an increased money flow.

Susie bought my book "Your Unconditioned Inner Magic" and used the contact email provided in the book to reach out to me. I worked with her for six weeks in group sessions and one-on-one. Susie recognised that previous relationships had been abusive and wanted to end the cycle of attracting abusive men. Many areas in her life didn't align with her desires. Susie had limiting beliefs and lacked self-love. She found herself avoiding any situation where there may be a confrontation. Susie would freeze up with anxiety and fear if any difficult conversations needed to be had. She enrolled in several courses and took on more than she could handle. Each time a course finished, she registered for another one, and the cycle continued. She was always the student and never the master. Susie would try and look for her self-worth in how many certificates she had.

Financially, Susie struggled to earn an income as a single mum and believed she couldn't find something that would work for her. However, her family was fortunate enough to supplement her income. This caused her to feel like she was a burden and a drain on her family, and she felt uncomfortable asking for money all the time. It caused her to feel a lot of shame and guilt. Susie also explained that no matter how much money was given to her, she was still short. She said it felt like there was a hole in her bank account, and the money just disappeared through it.

Neuroscience has proved that relationships shape our brains. Susie found working through her relationships particularly hard. She was determined to work through the exercises, and I supported her every step of the way. I remember confronting the Courts, Police and then speaking in the UK Parliament. I remembered the fear of having to address problems in my relationships with friends and family members. I could offer that support from a place of "knowing" and experience. Susie can now confidently have conversations she used to hide from. She has worked hard on her personal boundaries, stepped out of people-pleasing mode, and received her desired respect. Susie's relationships now flourish, and her relationship with herself has changed.

Susie had money problems, and her limiting beliefs prevented her from moving past them. Susie felt her life was a constant uphill struggle with debt mounting up, and there wasn't a job she could find that worked with her commitments as a mum. When Susie did have a job, she worked hard, but no matter how much she earned, her bank account was empty at the end of each month. What Susie didn't release is she was creating this version of her reality. Susie truly believed money has hard to earn, so it was hard to earn. That is what she was attracting in with her emotions. She could call on her parents anytime, but this money brought her guilt and shame. Susie couldn't hold money or reach above a certain amount in her bank accounts. Abundance is for everyone, but how do we accomplish this? Firstly, I taught Susie to follow the universal laws and do that inner work. Secondly, she needed to understand that where she was financially did not happen overnight, and where she is going won't happen overnight. However, she could be consistent in her change and growth. Susie began to understand she was where she was because of her previous mindset. The Mindset Exercises were challenging, but she didn't give up and now she experiences wealth in all areas.

We are the average of the five people who surround us, which is one of the keys I teach. Who is surrounding you? Krystal and

Susie were surrounded by negative people who believed life was hard and unfair, money would vanish into thin air, they were always in debt, they certainly didn't know how to hold money, and their relationships were chaotic and full of drama. Remember the saying, misery loves company? Our relationships are mirrors of ourselves, so it is crucial to find authentic, supportive people running in the same direction as you. One of the benefits of group sessions is that you will discover like-minded souls who are on the same path as you and want to connect.

If you are ready to take the next step just like Krystal and Susie did, email me or message me on Facebook. I am looking for people who want to grow and move forward. I will match your energy and inspire you to meet mine. Everyone's achievements will be celebrated. Your life is in your hands, and you are in the driver's seat.

Earl Nightingale once said, *"Most people tiptoe their way through life, hoping they make it safely to death."* I want you to think about this quote and ask yourself, do you agree?

I used to try and tiptoe my way through life, but that changed when my mindset did. I never wanted to confront or offend anyone. I always disliked the spotlight. But now I have found a new purpose, to serve from a place of abundance and wealth in all areas of my life. On the 17th of May 2023, I was invited to Parliament to speak about my experiences of "the system". I was failed time and time again, and I sought to change this experience for future generations. I now work towards changing legislation, policies and procedures and have had a national impact. I will continue working with the government and other organisations to advocate for the safety of others. Anything is possible when you believe it is.

Using my voice and platform has been a huge part of my healing journey, but it is spreading awareness and showing women how they can transform their lives after experiencing adverse experiences. My Podcast "Your Unconditioned Inner Magic" reminds me that I can talk authentically and push through my fears. You see, my perpetrator stalks me online with his friends. I speak my big ambitions aloud and share my dreams, knowing everything I do and say is being watched. Sometimes I feel very vulnerable, but I push through. Life after the abuse has been a considerable achievement for me, and my Podcast reminds me of this weekly. I am also incredibly honoured to have an outstanding line-up of guests who inspire, challenge and inform listeners. I actively look for people to interview. I aim to empower women and spread awareness.

I give listeners everything they need to rebuild a life with confidence and fortitude, from coping techniques for resiliency, tools to heal from trauma, exercises to develop a sense of self and teachings on utilising intuition, understanding patterns and behaviours, and ways to enjoy greater health, happiness and success. Get in touch if you would love to be interviewed on my next podcast episode.

As an international best-selling author, one of my goals is to continue writing and co-authoring. The first book I published is called "Your Unconditioned Inner Magic", and it is available on Amazon in all formats. I have never been so determined to share my story, help women and inspire. When I told my family I would write a book, they all gave me "that look". You see, I was struggling financially (but ironically was doing better than I ever had been), I am severely dyslexic, and I was a permanently sleep-deprived single mum whose son has Autism. When others didn't believe in me, I believed in me. And I wrote my first book in 3 months and sold over 800 copies in the first month and a half. I will never stop working to connect with like-minded women, to help them rediscover their passions, and equip themselves with the tools they need to overcome life's challenges. I want all generations and future ones to be emotionally healthy and safe. I want to teach women to put words to their emotions. I want to help women understand the power of their yes and the power of their no. I want to show them that we all can make mistakes but that they get to press reset and restart. If you are looking for someone to speak at your next event, reach out, my passion is to inspire, motivate and give hope to women who have been through adverse experiences, to bounce back and create a life that is full of meaning.

My lovely reader, thank you, let's connect. I would be honoured to get to know you.

Thank you for reading this chapter and for embarking on a journey of self-love. We are all connected, so my lovely reader, when I say I love you, I do.

"If we are related, we have, through these pages, met." - Napoleon Hill

Kitty O'Brien

About the Author

Kitty has a Diploma in Counselling, Early Years, Supporting Teaching in Schools, and Natural Healing. Kitty is also an international Author, Podcast Host and Motivational Speaker. Kitty advocates for domestic abuse and coercive control survivors through Parliament and is a proud single mum to her beautiful son, Harrison.

Through empowerment, clarity, and guidance, Kitty helps women find their soul calling. She has helped many women experience their own unique transformation and create a life that's barely recognisable to them.

In her spare time, Kitty hosts Psychic Events and private Psychic Readings. She also loves to explore Nature with her son and is involved with Re-Wilding Projects.

Email: contact@kittyobrien.com
Linktree: linktr.ee/kittyobrien
Website: www.kittyobrien.com

Justine Oldfield

Surviving a Covert Narcissist "Friend"

Slugs and snails and puppy dogs tails

That's what little boys are made of

Sugar and spice and all things nice

That's what little girls are made of.

Narcissistic abuse

We are brought up with poems like this and stories about how abusive men and boys can be. And somehow, told women are all lovely. The nurturers, the mothers, the carers, the best friends, the supporters, the kind empathic ones.

As we get older, we see in movies, news stories, documentaries, and personal experiences the truth can be vastly different.

Experts in personality disorders used to say narcissists were 80% male and 20% female. Now they are saying it's 50/50. Due to social media and many other factors. I think, like anything, we are just learning more every day. And it has always been this way, women just hide it and manipulate much better. Google is not up to date and simplifies narcissism entirely. Women are just more likely to be covert or even vulnerable narcissists, yes there are different kinds. They know how to act perfectly in public whilst doing terrible things behind closed doors. Nobody but those closest would have any idea they are abusive. Acquaintances think they are great! So, if the person being abused speaks up nobody believes them. All part of the abuser's plan from day one.

There has been a lot of talk about narcissism the last few years. Some people even say the term is overused. Experts on narcissism will assure it's not! And if you have not had a run in with one yet, brace yourself it's coming. Or of course you could be the narcissist! Completely dismissive of the entire subject because it describes you. Something to think about! LOL Or you may be one of the lucky ones, but even that I would find hard to believe. Every person I have never met has had a situation with an abusive person, whether at work, a family member, a daughter, son or a friend's relationship. All abusive people will have a cluster B personality disorder of some kind. Healthy people do not hurt others on purpose.

Even Dr Phil has done podcasts on the subject called Phil in the Blanks. Which is great, he too says it's a lot more common than people think, depending on where you live. He says by the nature of the area, for instance 50% of Hollywood will be Narcissists. And of course if you think about it. The shameless self-promotion. The attention seeking film industry, it's obvious. We have words for abusive people now that is the difference. Sam Vaknin a diagnosed Narcissist (Narcissistic personality disorder) is one of the most popular specialists on the subject, and coined the phrase Narcissistic abuse, he describes as total abuse; the aim is to kill you mentally. There are so many brilliant experts on the subject, some are psychologists, others are survivors that have lived it! Then gone on to research themselves and help others recover, like me.

My favourite experts on narcissism are, Dr Ramani, Ross Rosenberg, Christine Louis De Canonville, Les Carter, Lisa A Romano, Paula D'arcy, Dr Todd Grande, Lise Leblanc, HG Tudor, Sam Vaknin, Dr Phil, Danish Bashir, Richard Grannon, to name a few. And when I say favourites I mean I have watched hundreds of hours of their videos!

Christine in particular is incredible, she teaches psychologists about narcissism, and how to treat people recovering from them. This is not a normal break up, these people try to ruin your life. Narcissists are brilliant actors and liars, they fool phycologists too. I have known them to even be in romantic relationships with each other. It didn't end well. In fact, every relationship with a narcissist ends horrifically.

It's not as simple as being told to be positive and focus on the future. These survivors have been blindsided, conned, slandered, financially abused, and lied to in court, children taken from them. Some of the men I have helped have been lied about so much they were sent to prison. Men in particular find it very difficult to talk about abuse from their partners because we hear so much about domestic violence being a women's problem. A lot of people find it difficult to believe women can be so toxic. It starts with little put downs, nothing is ever good enough, then it escalates. Not always to violence. Most narcissists don't use violence at all. Psychological abuse is a slow insidious dismantling of your soul. Chinese water torture. Emotional rape. The gaslighting alone is enough to send somebody into a psychotic break. Narcissistic abuse is so dangerous it can drive people to suicide.

Narcissists have no boundaries. They only care about ruining the lives of anyone that doesn't accept or goes along with their delusional lives. The only friends they can maintain are known as flying monkeys in psychology. The term was named after The Wizard of Oz, where the witch is the narcissist and the flying monkeys she trained, groomed to do her dirty work. They are often not emotionally intelligent or narcissistic themselves. But a narcissist is just as brilliant at grooming allies as targets.

But if they know that the narcissist is toxic, lies, bullies, but they are either too scared to speak up because they will be in the firing line themselves or just don't care. They are the school bullies that never grew up. Narcissism is formed in childhood. Children that are not taught empathy, never held accountable, or they have a narcissist parent, so they learn that being underhanded bullies gets them what they want. Being a decent person is too much like hard work. Female narcissists know it is not socially acceptable to act this way in adulthood, so they build a false self which is usually extremely charming and nice. It's all a con!

That's when you really know you are dealing with someone with a personality disorder. They gather others to turn on you. They tell lies about you, often feigning concern. This can start weeks before the smear campaign, little lies to turn others against you, or doubt your credibility. All while saying things like "I'm trying my best to help her." It is often called hidden abuse. Covert narcissists are considered the most dangerous because they act like they care while trying to destroy their chosen target.

Meeting...

A new life. A new town. A new school for my children.

2010 I walked my sons to a new school. The anticipation, they were nervous, we were all settling into a new life in a town, and we knew nobody.

A couple of weeks in, I asked my son's teacher if there were any mum's groups or get togethers, to make new friends. She was a friendly lady with a good, straightforward, honest way about her. Straight away she called a few of the other mums over to introduce me. "These ladies all meet at the local park, they have a fun time!" They all made me feel very welcome to come along.

In no time I was invited to all their get togethers and (the one) was inseparable from another girl, they were always together. Which I thought was great and thought they were all lovely! I was so happy to have made friends so easily in such a tough time.

We all had children at the same school, and became good friends. Life seems wonderful for a few months. Then the girl she was closest to had a fall out with another mum in our circle. And the narrative flipped very quickly! The other mums could see both sides and tried to defuse the situation. But (the narcissist) escalated the situation, turned on her closest friend completely. I was trying to reason with her, trying to make the peace. She was completely dismissive and didn't speak to this lady again. Which now I see as another red flag. Even after and weeks of us trying to make her see it was just a misunderstanding, and she is still a good friend, she still refused to make peace. In a narcissist's/sociopath's mind you are either all good or all bad, they have black and white thinking. There is no understanding. To her she was gone. But little did I know at the time, she was no longer needed. It was all a ruse as she had another target in mind. Me.

In no time she was messaging me daily. Always making plans, saying how much we had in common. She was so fun! And of course, I was new to town, knew no one. A perfect target. Another red flag.

In the back of my mind, was always her last best friend she dismissed so quickly, they were inseparable when we first met. The first thing that did not sit right with me. Narcissists jump from friend to friend and have a string of ex's that they stay in contact with in case someone else falls through. This can be mistaken as fun and resilience, but the fact is they don't attach to people and are incapable of love. Every relationship in their lives is transactional. They are the lead actors and everyone else is the bit parts. If you do not play your part, or call them out on their bad behaviour you are gone!

We had so much fun for around 3 years before she unravelled. Everything I liked she liked! (another red flag-mirroring/the love bombing stage, yes friends do it too). We were literally inseparable, we did everything together. She would text me whilst getting our children ready for school. Sometimes 20-30 times, another red flag. At the time I was flattered. I thought she just loved me. No, it's all part of the trap.

Two years went by and two mutual friends caught her lying. I got a phone call from one, she told me to come over asap. I did and she explained how she told one of our friends a completely different story than what she told us. And it wasn't a silly little lie. It was about the birth of her child. We were in shock. We all were! The friend said I would have never had believed it in a million years. We discussed bringing it up, but she said let's just watch her and see how this pans out. Nothing happened. But we never trusted her fully after that.

Another girl was introduced to our circle. She seemed nice. But a little stand offish. She started coming out with us a lot and was a bit angry as her ex had cheated on her and she was on a weight loss mission to get a revenge body, so she said.

I honestly thought we were all friends. All very different but all friends. But I knew we couldn't trust her. She was nasty about her other friends and said things like 'my daughter is just like me, she isn't a bitch, she just cares about her friends so much she comes off aggressively.' Hmmm apple and tree springs to mind... Another red flag. There was no kindness or empathy. But I didn't spend much time with her, so it didn't bother me as others in the group did.

This is where the devaluation stage began. The second stage and pattern of behaviour of every narc/sociopath. Just like her previous best friend. She had spotted her next target. My time was up. Another red flag. I was lied to and gaslighted. For example, I was told we were going out on Friday, "I will pick you up at 7pm", Then told it had changed to Saturday. Saturday morning they would post the night out on Facebook. When I confronted my best friend she would say things like "no I told you! You got it wrong." Gaslighting, lying to deny your reality to make you seem unhinged. Then she would smirk and say "are you ok?" Another huge narc/sociopath red flag.

Lies. Gossip. Putting people down, often as soon as they turned their backs. Mocking and haughty behaviour. Saying she stayed in, then others saying she was out. Then lying about it. Sleeping with anyone she could. Flirting with any guy she came in contact with, including friend's husbands, or partners. It was like I never knew her. She went from this nice, kind girl into a monster before my eyes.

She was messaging my father in the UK, saying I wasn't well and she was worried about me! She said, "you are like my second father." Just wow who tries to turn your own parents against you? He knew this was very strange as my father and I were very close. There is no way he would believe anyone else on earth over me. But this is how delusional they are!

One of the worst things she did. I had said months ago to my bestie we should take our kids to Hawaii. She agreed and seemed really excited. And I told my kids we were planning it. She said she wouldn't tell her kids yet. Months later after us discussing it many times. She posted on Facebook a video of her and this new girl and all their kids. The children were lined up on the sofa, and they said to them 'what are we doing today kids?' They replied, 'going to school.' She said, 'no you are not, you are packing your suitcases because we are all going to HAWAII!!!' But this was posted 3 days before I ever saw it, she had blocked me then unblocked me 3 days later. So, 1, I looked like I wasn't congratulating them and seemed to be some sort of hater and 2, I couldn't go to her house because they were already there. So, you can imagine I was less than happy! It was so hurtful, all our mutual friends, teachers at our children's school congratulating them, saying things like you guys are the best mums ever! When in reality they are backstabbing snakes. I am not sure if the other girl that went in my place knew it was my idea, as narcissists love to not tell the full story. But if she did, she is as bad as the narcissist. Not only did it break my heart but my children's too. This is just a small example of her behaviour, there are hundreds more!

That was the beginning of the end! I was done.

My closest friend was a total fraud.

Tables turn

One day I was driving my girls and they were arguing I was heading around a corner, in a split second I considered driving straight, straight into a tree and ending it all. The pain and stress was indescribable. I snapped awake and swerved to save us all.

I drove to a safe spot and cried for 5 minutes straight. My girls were only about 9 and 7 and were crying and we were all hugging. I dried my tears, and something changed in me. I wasn't going to let a Pathological dangerous covert narc/sociopath end my life and leave my children motherless. I was ready to fight back!

My friend is a psychologist, I told her what was happening, and she told me to research NPD, narcissistic personality disorder. I was so shocked, she had every single trait and pattern of behaviour. I was horrified. I was like finding aliens exist and she was your closest friend! I went to see another psychologist to make sure this was true, and she agreed I'd been targeted –in her words, "by someone extremely dangerous and definitely has NPD or psychopathy." She said "there is absolutely nothing wrong with you and this is a normal reaction to pathological abuse. "

I started asking questions on Quora about narcissistic behaviour, a few weeks in I was asked a question and it snowballed! I kept being asked for more, over 450 000 people have read my content there, then a friend suggested I do an Instagram page, I was asked to do interviews on podcasts. Then asked to work with a LA charity helping survivors recover. Then I did a Facebook page. And private online recovery coaching all over the world helping hundreds of people.

The future

I am just extremely lucky and grateful to be alive. It was not without cost. My whole family suffered. It took years to feel safe again. I'll never be the same. I can't trust like I used to. I over analyse. I spot red flags everywhere!

The lesson. Be incredibly careful who you let into your life. Healthy people take time to get to know you. Yes, I wanted new friends. I was too trusting and in a vulnerable position. I could never have dreamt what happened to me. But it does happen to kind, trusting, empathic people every single day. And no, it does not make me or anyone else naive or foolish. These people are predatory, seek out people they admire so they can learn from you, steal your good ideas and traits to fool others down the track. Then as time goes by, they begin to hate you because they possess no good qualities, and they begin to despise you and want you gone. Narcissists are perpetually bored, and need to move on to a new supply because either you realise, they are disordered, or they find a new target.

But hey! What doesn't kill you...

There is hope! You can recover and thrive! And learn strategies to spot and repel them. All things I teach online video calls worldwide.

I am happy, healed and loving life. And looking forward to my next exciting chapter

I will carry on helping others recover. More podcasts. Seminars with other survivors in the pipeline. And boy this would make a brilliant movie!

Loving my family and friends.

Love Justine. x

About the Author

Justine Oldfield is a single mother of four beautiful children. Born in the UK, grew up in New Zealand and Australia, back to the UK at 13 then emigrated back to Queensland in 2006. She resides on the stunning Sunshine Coast. Where she will be found walking her Mini Dachshund Boo on the pristine beaches.

A mother, friend, worldwide traveller, advocate for domestic violence and narcissistic abuse survivors, writer and recovery coach.

Achievements, worked with a nonprofit organisation in the US coaching people recovering from Narcissistic abuse. Done podcasts and interviews on Narcissism. Writes about recovery and has helped hundreds of people worldwide recover from Narcissistic abuse. Not a bad mum, apparently! lol

@ Quora Justine Oldfield
Facebook, Instagram: @narcbuster2020
Email: justineoldfield@hotmail.co.uk

Dr Angie Papas-Ginis

"To change my world I have to change myself. To change myself I have to stop my world; When I stop my world I can change myself and when I can change myself I can change my world"

The day I woke up from my life everything changed. It was like a hurricane that came in, threw everything up in the air, mixed it all up and spat them back down. Now it was up to me to sort them out, fix and keep what was valuable, and everything that was broken had to be thrown away. How did I get here? Was I asleep for so long even though my eyes were wide open? No! This didn't just happen. So many questions going around in my head! Why didn't someone wake me up?

You might be asking what am I referring to? I am talking about the life journeys we take, thinking we are on the right path, the path that leads us to salvation.

My path was carved on the side of the mountain the day I was born and have been climbing that mountain with bleeding hands, stone by stone, because nobody told me that there's a well-lit road on the other side of the mountain, leading all the way to the peak.

What happened to me the last five decades? Just like so many, I created stories about my past experiences, and these stories created havoc in my life. We go through every day believing those stories, and then we interpret our experiences according to the meaning we give to those events. We are continuously faced with obstacles and struggles we blame others for and occasionally ourselves, or we blame it on fate and we move on only to experience more of the same.

Until one day somebody comes along, or you read a book, or listen to a podcast, to show you a different way of looking at how you do things, how you talk to yourself, how you criticise yourself and others, how your mindset controls you and suddenly there's a hurricane at your doorstep.

So many of us suffer daily because we haven't become aware of the subconscious conditioning controlling our very thoughts, our very words and our very actions. I am who I want to Be. The change that I want to see in the world needs to start from me. I am responsible for my life and therefore my happiness. I have attracted everything that has happened to me. These are the mottos that I live by these days. It wasn't always the case. I lived in fear, shame, pain and regret most if not all of my life, until 3 years ago, when I had an awakening.

It wasn't an instant transformation, but going into different personal development avenues, I learnt to ask myself different questions about who I truly was and what and who had shaped me.

Growing up in a severely dysfunctional family, exposed constantly to mental and physical abuse(constant beatings), forced me to wear a mask, in order to hide my pain and my shame for my family. I wanted to have a normal life, like so many around me. I gained strength and hope from the love and acceptance I was receiving from outsiders, schoolfriends, teachers, neighbours. The mask allowed me to integrate into the world, without anyone knowing how broken I was on the inside. I believed that if I held on till, I was 18 years old, I would be able to escape that hell I was in.

In a way I was right, but in so many ways I was so wrong. It took me up to the age of 54 to really escape the inferno I was in. I was oblivious to the chains that were around me, connecting and keeping me prisoner to my past.

Life-threatening experiences and torment, pushed me into a personal war that would last decades: I was not worthy enough, because I was not loved and treasured by the two people that mean the world to a child: my parents.

I was born in Athens, Greece in 1966 and didn't permanently migrate to Sydney, Australia until I was 15 years old. My memories of those years are filled with fear, pain, agony, and shame. My life story is too long and complex to include it all in this chapter, so I will try to give a very short synopsis. My father was a very brutal man, that abused his family physically and mentally. Every day we would all live in fear as the smallest thing could trigger him and cause him to explode. My mother and my older sister were the ones affected the most, as they ended up in hospital several times from my father's beatings. Times were different 50 years ago when it came to such abuse; domestic violence was not a topic to be dealt with by the authorities. Even though my mother was aware of all the horrible things my father was doing, she felt hopeless in taking her kids and leaving. So, the disharmony continued even when we came to Australia. My father was totally controlled by money and even though he wasn't rich by any means, the money that he did have, he will not share it with us. He would provide a roof over our heads, bare, minimal food and recycled clothes; we had to beg for days just to get some books and pencils for our school. I received my first present from my father (for any occasion, that is, birthday, Christmas etc) when I was 19 years old and that's because he had won it at the RSL club! We, as a family never experienced presents under the tree, or birthday parties. As the years multiplied, so did my scars, but my mask was hiding them so well, that not many people realised what was going on.

The fear, the pain the misery that I was feeling every day, were fuelling my inner strength to keep on going. I excelled at school, both in Greece and when I came to Australia. I believed it was going to be my way out of this inferno I was living in. I stay focused on my dream of freedom, of normality, of joy, of happiness. I observed people and families around me and the fact that I could see normality in their lives, then I knew normality was waiting for me too; the day I would leave my destructive, unsafe home environment was in the horizon.

The toxicity at home continued for years; I was too embarrassed to face the neighbours that could hear the screams and the fights coming from my home. Was my self-esteem affected? Absolutely. My father made sure to let us know every day that we were meant for nothing, that we will be nothing, that we needed him and that especially us girls, will always need a man to protect them and guide them in life. Because of all that embedded in my head, I lived in deception about who I was: circumstances had misguided me to accept beliefs about me and what I truly deserved. I thought I loved myself, but boy was I wrong.

I was so fortunate to find people around me that gave me love, hope, strength and when I was with them, I forgot about everything. When I was 15 years old I was fortunate to live next to the person who became my best friend, my confident, the one who accepted me as I was, even though she knew the truth about me and my family- she pushed me to keep on going, to never give up on my dreams and to keep believing that my life was meant for more. To this day we are still best friends, as we are each other's yin and yang, and she hasn't stopped encouraging me to chase after my goals.

My 18th birthday came around, but I didn't open the door to escape, as I knew that if I did that, my father would literally kill my mother, as he blamed everything on her. So, I stayed, learnt to harness that hate for my father into fuel that propelled me forward: I wasn't going to give up, I was going to prove him wrong.

Even when I was accepted into Sydney University to do Dentistry, but father simply said to me: "You got in, let me see how you are going to get out…" -no congratulations, no I am proud of you, no nice words at all. As all 18-19 years old and being at university, I wanted to go out with my friends and fellow students, but that was impossible. My father was insanely strict, I could not even be an hour late coming back from Uni, there would be WW3. I was getting so depressed, that I thought I would never be able to escape this inferno, so on my 21st birthday, the warrior inside me vanished and I tried to commit suicide; ending up in hospital, taught me a lesson: I have a life to live and I need to take responsibility in how I am going to live it- But how would I do that?

I left home, managed to live with a fellow student and her kind family, only for a while, as she stopped going to University and went overseas; of course that forced me to move out and without any financial support, I had to move back home.

My parents decided to relocate back to Greece, with my older sister and her family, leaving behind my brother and I. During that time my brother, was newlywed but incapacitated, as he was in a tragic car accident, that put him in hospital for 3 months and years of medical interventions, and I was still studying dentistry. My parents, not caring at all, decided to return to Greece, leaving my brother and I struggling to survive financially- absolutely no support from them at all. I was having instant noodles, Monday to Friday at university, as that was the cheapest thing that I could buy. My brother and I became extremely close, and it was that love for each other and the love and support we received from so many people around us that got us through those hard times. We both managed to finish our degrees, feeling stronger than ever but being tormented internally everyday by the experiences we had lived through and the indifference from our parents.

I got married straight after my graduation, because as my father's words were imbedded in my head, I needed a man to look after me. I had so much anger, resentment and hate inside for my father and what had happened all those years, that I started to hate myself as well and be super critical of everything I did. It didn't take long, for all that negativity to affect my body and within a short time, I was diagnosed with a tumour in my head.

I didn't want to believe the diagnosis! I was so miserable: I was in a loveless marriage, hating dentistry as I was working nearly 50 hours a week and feeling as though there was no hope, no way out! As the medication was ineffective, my specialist suggested surgery. Prior to the due date, I attended Anthony Robbins (the personal transformational guru) seminar, that I had felt compelled to go. I will forever feel grateful for that day, because it helped me to find my hope again. I went into that operating theatre believing that all would be well, and the new me would emerge on the other side. Yes, all went well, except for the fact that they could not remove all of the tumour and that meant that besides taking medication for the rest of my life, I may never be a mum. When my surgeon told me that, I heard him but decided not to believe him. I knew deep down that my day will come. And through more obstacles,

more mountains that I had to climb, more heartache and a second marriage, my gorgeous boy, Nikolas, entered my world in 2000.

We believe that parents are there to support their kids but, I was convinced, my son was there to keep my heart beating, to hold my hand and guide me along my journey.

Life continued from that day, with me trying to find who I was, to let go of the chains holding me back to my past, but even though I believed I was progressing, looking back now, I was always living in my past, believing I was a victim. I wanted to please everyone around me, I wanted to be perfect at everything, I wanted my life to be perfect. And in search for perfection, I lost myself even more. We blame life for throwing at us obstacles and struggles, but it is us that actually attract all these into our world. A great transformational teacher (Jim Fortin) taught me-just recently, that "Life doesn't test Us, Life reflect Us". Even though I had embraced personal development from the age of 25, what I was telling myself and what I was feeling in my core, were two completely different things. I was wishing for change but to do that we need to change who we are now! I was sailing through my storm, blaming the storm, and not realising that I had decided to go through it, I had decided to stay stuck in my past. The shame and the hate that I had for myself, blinded me from seeing my way through that storm.

My internal unhappiness continued for years, trying to read and listen to everything about personal development, in order for someone or something to show me a way out of this emptiness I was feeling. I criticised myself all day long, asking whether I behaved the right way, said the right words, dressed appropriately, showed too much emotion, too little emotion, was I a good student, was I a good dentist, was I was a good employer, was I a good girlfriend, wife, mother, friend, and the list went on and on.

My brother's unexpected death in 2011, was a cruel wake-up call for me. I felt that all the heartache that I had experienced up to that point in my life was nothing compared to what I felt, standing there, without Him being next to me. Everyone was seeing a warrior on the exterior but my inner being was shot to pieces. And those pieces were brought back to me piece by piece by those around me, my family and closest friends that, without most of them knowing, held them for me until I was ready to put them back together again.

I knew there was a superwoman in me, as she had fought to keep me afloat through my childhood years, she suppressed some of my pain, so I could breathe and smile, fool everyone around me that my life was perfect:

but even her strength would be defeated by my insecurities. I owe this warrior a lot, as she dragged me away from despair when I came out of my suicide, when I had nothing to eat, nowhere to sleep, no money to buy my university books, helped me overcome my illness and held my hand going through so so many hurdles! Yes, I owe her my survival but somehow, I forgot to show her my gratitude.

Following the death of my brother, and when I eventually woke up from the mental trauma that it caused me, I vowed to find that superwoman, to find my dharma, to liberate myself from the past, to find peace and finally to set out achieving my goals. As the saying goes: "when the student is ready, the teacher appears", my teacher appeared just at the right moment in my life, at the beginning of 2020. Just as the world started living in fear because of Covid, I started letting go of my internal fears and limitations. Because of the questions he forced me to ask of myself, I finally realised where all the blockages where, what was really holding be back from discovering the real me and achieving the success I had dreamed about since I was a little girl.

I had filled my life with band-aids in order to hide my insecurities: I tried to achieve more and more, love more, give more. NO didn't exist in my vocabulary-it was replaced by, Yes: I will do whatever you ask, just as long as you will love me and accept me. I believed that the image that I was building externally would somehow cancel out what I was feeling inside. I was living through a set of memorized stories and emotions, all evolving from my history and those feelings were defining who I was: unworthy, unlovable. I fed my insecurities with more learning about how to be successful as a woman, more information on personal development, how to empower those around me and especially women. But then we reach a point that no matter how much knowledge we consume, it doesn't numb the pain or the emptiness we feel within.

My second marriage ended in 2020, a month or so before the world went into lockdown due to Covid. I could see where we went wrong, but also how we grew apart. Even though the sadness was there, for the first time in my life, I could see clearly. I could see where my roadblocks had been, I could see the chains holding me attached to the little girl in my past, I knew why the obstacles had appeared repeatedly, and at the same time, I realised what I had to do. I can't tell you that it was one specific thing that turned me around, but when I had the time to spend with myself, and ask those questions that dig deep, that make you shed so many layers, that you think there's nothing left of the old you, my transformation began.

The transformational coach that forced me to look hard at the mirror, at that time, was the right teacher that I needed at that phase of my life to pull out of my abyss.

I began to embrace my imperfections, let go of self-judgement, learnt to explore the power of forgiveness but above all I learnt to cultivate self-love. My journey is not over, but I have finally let go of my past, kept the lessons it has taught me, learnt to accept me, value me, celebrate the woman that I am and every day I feel more and more gratitude for waking up not living in fear, but rather in peace; it's an emotion that in my 57 years I have never experienced.

I have achieved so much in my personal and professional life, just in these 3 years, and I know it's because for the first time, I value me, I accept me, I love me.

I am so excited for what tomorrow will bring but I could not be here without the survivor in me and the love that I have received and continue to receive from my dearest friends and family: I will be forever grateful!

About the Author

Angie is a dentist of 33 years, having graduated from Sydney University. She is a national and international speaker on dental lasers; she has completed her Masters in Laser Dentistry from LA&HA Institute in Slovenia, Masters in Laser Science from Catholic University in Rome, awarded the Lifetime Achievement Award (Global Summit Institute), and has been accepted in the prestigious Pierre Fauchard Academy, a fellowship that marks the distinction that demonstrates her commitment to lifelong learning to her patients and her peers.

She is the founder of Dentistry By Women, a platform of empowerment for women in dentistry. Angie's passion doesn't only lie with Dentistry but also with helping women find their voices, their self-worth and self-love. She is currently living and practicing dentistry in Sydney, Australia.

Email: drapapas21@gmail.com
Facebook: https://www.facebook.com/angie.papasginis
Instagram: @angiepapasginis

Lorette Parrillo

Reflecting on Linear Time – Countin down the days Or makin the days count!

Tick Tock, Tick Tock ….. 4 AM and I'm wide awake looking at the clock on my night table. Ever have one of those nights? I can't fall back to sleep, so I use this opportunity to take a trip down memory lane. I'm inviting you to come with me.

It all began in the 1950's. Like many others in the 1950's, my parents had a dream of how they wanted their life to go. They planned many things, most of which never came to pass. After marrying, they moved from New York to Florida. Had two children, spaced ideally – two years apart. A boy and then a girl. The so called 'perfect little family.' They bought their own little home in Miami with a small yard for their children to grow up and play in. They were focused on giving the best life possible to their offspring, just as we all are. Life seemed ideal for them at that moment in time.

Their dreams began to unravel when my mother was diagnosed with breast cancer. She struggled with that for many years (much of that time is a blur to me as I was so young and only focused on the things small children usually focus on; like playing with friends and watching TV). During that time period, my father passed away quite suddenly of a massive heart attack at the young age of 42! A 'widow maker' heart attack which surprised so many! It was very unexpected and left my mother totally devastated. What was she to do now? A young widow with cancer and two small children to raise. No life insurance and no real savings. She had no skills, as many women of that time period just stayed home to raise their children. From somewhere deep inside her, she summoned the strength to go on. I didn't know it at the time, but this innerspring of strength was passed on to me and enabled me to withstand many of my own tribulations later on in life.

My mother did the only thing she was qualified to do at the time. She knocked on neighbor's doors and offered her services for cleaning homes and for babysitting. She knocked on many a door and was able to find a few people willing to give her a try. She was a hard worker and even while sick she kept an immaculate home. I suppose she channeled that energy into cleaning. Against all odds, she was quite successful with her little 'maid jobs' and was able to support my brother and I as we grew up into teenagers. We certainly didn't live a life of luxury—but neither did we want for anything. I will always love and respect her so much for that!

Many times the doctors told her sisters (my aunts) to make plans for us as she wouldn't live on, but she defied them and all the odds and she successfully raised us until at the age of 19, I then lost my beautiful mother. The cancer had traveled through the years throughout her entire body, and at this point it was in her pancreas and there was nothing more to be done. I felt so alone that day when I lost my mother. But somewhere inside me I knew … Yes, I had lost a mother but I had gained a guardian angel. This realization would follow me throughout the hardest times in my life.

Now I was all alone in the world. My only brother had turned to drugs as a way of coping with the stress of our father's passing, our mothers' illness and eventual passing. He was barely coping. He chose to live his own special kind of hell that we were all powerless to break him out of. The life of an addict is not a pleasant one; neither for them or for their loved ones. He had not inherited that innerspring of strength from my mother as I had. Fortunately, I did have a close relationship growing up with my mother's fraternal twin sister, my Aunt Ana. She became even more of a second mother to me during that time and up until her death many years later. But still, many times I felt alone and confused and angry and scared all at the same time. How was my future life going to be?

It certainly hadn't started out very well in my opinion! Despite all this going on at the time, I managed to get a bachelor's degree from a reputable local college while maintaining a 3.8 grade point average. Now to begin my life.

It was also during this time period, I met the man who was to become my future husband and the father of my two children. He wasn't what I was normally attracted to or envisioned for myself, but he was handsome enough and I was drawn to the 'old fashioned' stability of him and his nuclear family. He was the oldest of 8 children and I loved their family dynamic. Something I was sorely missing in my upbringing. No fault of my parent's of course. Just a missing piece that I wanted; family stability. So we married in June of 1978 and life went on.

Just like my parents before me, we made plans for the life we envisioned for ourselves. What we wanted to do, have and be. We settled in Florida and bought our own home which was very nice, with a pool and a yard. Nice neighborhood near my 'special' aunt. Lots of fruit trees. The "American dream". We started our family. Two children, both boys. As the days turned into weeks, months and years; I felt something was wrong. Something was missing. What was missing? ME. The 'real me' was missing. I wasn't able to do what resonated and be who I really was in that marriage. Part of the reason being my husband at the time had gravitated towards being involved in a religious 'cult'. For a time he had me also involved. Later I realized it was not what I wanted to be a part of. My soul called to me to leave. To look for and pursue my own larger purpose. So when my youngest son was 16 years old, I packed my bags and left. I felt a lot of guilt over that at the time. Now I was on my own again. I was frightened but determined to succeed. I climbed the corporate career ladder for many years. I landed a coveted job with a fortune 100 company and was a top notch sales person, winning many awards and accolades, as well as president club trips. I should have been thrilled with my life at that time. But I wasn't. Don't get me wrong, there were times I was very happy and excited during that time period. But again, something was missing. ME.

Over the years, I kept looking for 'my purpose' in life. What am I doing here? What is God's intention for me? I was a generous person who donated quite regularly to various causes and charities dear to my heart. I helped people in need as much as possible. I was always focused on helping my two sons as much as possible, even as they became grown men. They were (and are) the center of my world; my most important legacy to this earth. Like all parents, I wanted them to be happy in life. And like all parents, I was powerless to ensure this. I had to learn (and am still learning) that each of us has our own journey to undertake here on this planet we temporarily reside upon. We cannot force others into our vision for them. Each soul must undertake their own journey in their own way.

Fast forward and I met another man later in life. Someone who I connected with both on a friendship level, as well as a romantic partner. He seemed to be the ideal partner I'd been searching for. He felt the same way about me. About 5 years later, we married in November of 2014. We are still together, although we've had our share of ups and downs, as all marriages do. We had said in our vows, 'for better or for worse' and we've been through both. And will probably continue to. I also continued working full-time in stressful, demanding corporate jobs that I did not resonate with at all. I was successful in terms of my positions with my employers and financially. But again, something was missing. ME. I dreaded getting up in the morning and going to work at a job I did not care for. Buying things I didn't need to impress people who didn't really matter. Even though I made a lot of money at that time, I still was living paycheck to paycheck, I felt so trapped on the hamster wheel of life. Something had to give.

Fast forward again until now. The day of the "Line in the sand" arrived when I was planning for my long awaited retirement. I'd worked so hard for so long and didn't have a lot to show for it. What was I going to do once I retired? Both health and finances came to mind. How could I afford to live the type of lifestyle I'd always dreamed of as a retiree? I didn't see a way. Social security alone was not going to cut it. The bulk of my 401K savings had been decimated during the brutal stock market crash of 2007/2008 which was a part of that recession at the time. I was never fully able to recoup my losses due to various personal reasons; but needless to say, it was very deflating and depressing at the time. My "golden years" suddenly didn't look so golden. And the impact I wanted to make on the planet? The philanthropist I wanted to become? The travel and adventure I wanted to pursue? Making sure my children were taken care of once I'm no longer here? These were all going through my mind. What could I do to ensure all these boxes were checked? I saw no way. A very scary and frustrating time for me.

Eagerly anticipating my long awaited retirement, I had plans that I wanted to be able to put into place. I have now since retired from the corporate world, and here's what I'm doing .... I joined a gym and regularly work out there three times a week. I now eat healthy, organic foods and I cook from home a lot more often. I drink lots of my fabulous, healthy 9.5 PH hydrogenized, ionized water daily. Best water on the planet! I've truly become a 'water snob'. lol My newfound healthier lifestyle has given me so much more energy to really enjoy retired life!

I donate regularly to many charities and causes that I'm aligned with. These are near and dear to my heart. It bothers me that I'm not currently able to do more with them. I'm looking forward to the day when I can add a few extra zero's onto my donations! I'm envisioning it all.... And I am also adding in some Volunteer Time now that I'm retired!

I now study many subjects which are of interest to me. Particularly Self development. I read and watch videos, I study, I meditate, I pray, I reflect, I walk my dog in nature daily.

I've also become a student of 'ancient wisdom teachings' as well. These ageless wisdom teachings are an ancient body of spiritual teachings underlying ALL scientific, social and cultural achievements, as well as many of the world's religions. This has really resulted in my being able to look at life through the 'bigger picture' of things. Not so wrapped up in the day to day. Realizing that we are truly all One and interconnected in the fabric of the Universe. This has not replaced my spiritual views, rather it has enhanced them. Fear has permeated so much of society nowadays (now more than ever). Fear creates suffering and blocks. It keeps us from becoming who we truly are. We must move from mind to heart to have this new consciousness. It is always a work in progress.

So I then asked the Universe. Show me the way. Show me what's next? I've been searching for so long and I need guidance now. What appeared afterwards in my Facebook feed was a happy, smiling woman who posted about a business and a lifestyle I envisioned for myself. One of self care, travel, and abundance in every way. I wanted to know more. I reached out. The rest is history. I am now in that business myself. I took inspired action towards my dream lifestyle. I joined an online home based business which checks all the boxes. Time freedom, location freedom, and money freedom. The best part is as I am living my best life now, I get to also help other women who are in the same boat I was in. I get to show them the way to time, location, and money freedom as well. I'm so happy and blessed that the Universe answered my query that day. I had an unwavering belief in myself and that I was destined for more than what I was seeing show up in my life. Perhaps you have felt that way too?

I've discovered along my journey that the most important thing is to be my authentic self. The good, the bad, and everything in between. There is no other way to be. Better to be my authentic self than a fake version of me designed to not "rock the boat" and please other people. The disapproval of some family and friends is something I've had to endure as I transformed from that conforming 'people pleaser' to being my true self. People ask me if it's worth it. It's all worth it. No regrets. I've learned, I've grown, and I've morphed into a better version of Me.

They say when people are very old and on their deathbeds, they are asked what they would change about their life or do differently. Almost all of them have been recorded as saying that they would enjoy life more, take more risks, do more things, and not be afraid. They would DO MORE! Fear would not stop them from enjoying Life more! No one said, "I'd put more time into my 9-5 corporate job!" This makes perfect sense to me now. Although for years, I was caught up in that 9-5 corporate world, just trying to get by and make ends meet. To live a life I thought I wanted. Turns out it wasn't the life I wanted at all.

Now, at last, as time keeps ticking on, I've finally found ME! The REAL me. The Me I've always wanted to be. I get to show up as **Me** every single day. I'm so grateful that now I get to choose exactly what I'd like to do, have and be each and every day! All while living the dream, helping others and the planet. **Making the days count**. It doesn't get much better than this!

About the Author

Lorette Parrillo is a wife, mother of two fabulous grown sons, currently living in the sunny hometown of St. Petersburg, Florida in the USA.

She is a successful sales executive and an accomplished sales trainer who has now retired from the corporate world.

Lorette enjoys cooking, fine dining, a nice glass of red wine on occasion, being out in nature, and spending time with friends and family – including her adored fur baby, Toby!

She is now involved in volunteer charity work; is a freedompreneur who is building a successful online business in high ticket affiliate marketing. Living her best life and assisting others to do the same!

Email: lortt123@gmail.com
Facebook: https://www.facebook.com/lortt2
LinkedIn: https://www.linkedin.com/in/lorette-parrillo-0a647615/

Emily Pettigrew

It was New Year's Eve 2014. I was sitting outside reflecting on the past year. It had been shit.

I was stuck, lost and empty.

I was 38 with two kids and in a 15-year relationship. And yet, I felt more alone than ever.

Mind you, things hadn't always been shitty. The early days were fun and carefree, partying hard; life wasn't taken too seriously. I was 22, he was 34. Before kids, we'd had some great times and some crappy times – like most relationships, I guess.

They say, "love is blind". I think it's because we choose to overlook certain things because we crave happiness - to have a companion, to matter to someone. Yes, I noticed the flaws in our relationship, but I also craved connection and a happy family life. So I overlooked the flaws. These wanted desires stopped me from accepting what was really going on.

Sometimes, we just see what we want to see; the things that make our ideal dream world seem achievable.

Hindsight can be great – in hindsight. But it cannot help us during the moments we are living at the time.

I thought; if I was a great mother, if I let things slide, kept the peace then he would love me the way I wanted to be loved. Naturally, the way we want to be loved changes as we change. It was tricky to balance wanting to remain an independent, strong woman and wanting to be nurtured by someone close.

So, New Years Eve, 2014, I found myself in deep reflection and realised that as people, our individual needs are constantly changing. My partner and I had forgotten to meet each other where we currently were. I was now 38 and yet, I felt like I was still being seen as the 22-year-old version of myself instead of the woman I actually was.

I was remembering all the times we fought. Neither of us had had role models that taught us how to communicate effectively, him with his outbursts and me clamming up. There were harsh, drunken, sarcastic digs at each other that baffled our friends because they could sense the truth in them. Then the blow-ups when my partner had been drinking his 'truth serum'. I realised I had been walking on eggshells with him for so long because I felt all he could see about me, were my pitfalls.

I was carrying a heavy burden of suppressed negative emotional energy and had been for a long while.

I wanted my home to be light and happy for my kids but it was becoming harder and harder to hold it together – I was slowly becoming just a husk of who I was, who I wanted to be and who I knew I was at my core.

In 2007, I embarked on my personal, spiritual journey – the beginnings of re-connection to myself, with the hope it would flow through into family life and my relationship. I pursued and achieved my Reiki Master certification, which in turn, increased the thirst I had for self-improvement and understanding myself. I thought; if I became a better person, then maybe I could be happy in our relationship. Despite gaining my certification and attending weekly spiritual development classes, the relationship worsened.

Hindsight reminded me that it takes two people in a relationship to do the work.

For the next seven years, I furthered my studies and immersed myself into Holistic Counselling and Complementary Therapies which gave me more insight into human traits, patterns and habits. I completed courses in NLP, communication skills and various healing modalities. I attended workshops, seminars – all in the hope of becoming happy and a better person for those around me.

Fast forward to NYE 2014 – and it finally landed:

For my life to be what I wanted it to be, I had to make myself happy.

I was waiting to be loved and desired by someone outside of me; waiting for them to see my worth, validate me and acknowledge the inner work I had been doing, which was in fact, actually working! However, it seemed my personal growth and change was actually making our relations worse instead of better. I was being blamed, shamed and guilt-tripped even more than before.

In the holding on to my dream of happy families and through my naivety - hoping that if I lead the way in self-improvement and change, then my partner might follow – it became more apparent that the chase towards my ideal, was becoming futile. He admitted he was unwilling to open his Pandora's box; to look inside and start to heal - because his own fears of drowning in overwhelm were too much for him to consider.

With this awareness, I realised I had to let go of the idea he was the villain and start to own my shit.

How could our relationship work when I seemed to be a huge trigger for him? We had talked, seen counsellors, and tried to make change – but nothing changed. All the awareness I had gained through my efforts to be happy slowly started to pull together. It was out of my control to make anyone else happy. That was on them. And so, I realised, it was on ME to make myself happy. That was in my control, choosing what helped me bloom. It was in my actions and reactions that would create my happiness and my life.

I had to start owning and admitting to myself that the fact that I was currently in this position, was because of the choices I had made along the way. I had chosen to keep quiet and keep the peace. I had chosen to put up with the verbal abuse that came with drunken nights. I had chosen to stay in the relationship for the sake of the kids, hoping that we would work it out and be the loving, happy family I wanted.

I also had to allow myself the grace of falling down because when I made those choices, I didn't have the resources or tools at the time, nor the courage or understanding to stand up for myself. Not like I have now.

I was doing what so many of us do; relying on the external world for validation and worth. I had given my power away; to him and others. And through this, I had lost myself.

The 2014 NYE was significant for me and I made a resolution for myself. I had to be the change. I had to be the one to take my power back and make some hard decisions. It was up to me. I had learnt more and gained more wisdom and now it was time to action it.

I had to step into the purpose of my self-discovery journey. I had to action my awareness to become aligned to the person I wanted to be. I had to start liking who I was without taking on other people's opinions of me as truth. I had to learn to trust myself in it all, to do what was right for me; not everyone else.

I had to finally decide. Leaving this relationship would be hard. Yet, I was already doing it hard, living in this toxic environment.

I was miserable.

I had to choose my hard.

Choosing to stay where I was scared the shit out of me. My Soul was dying.

Choosing to leave felt daunting, but it also glimmered with freedom.

I wanted more. I knew I was more.

And so I chose. Me.

My Soul danced with excitement as I chose to pursue the journey of Self Mastery.

This is the journey I continue today, and I choose to share my learnings with others through my work.

Here's a snapshot of my basic foundations for Self – Mastery.

1. Know your self – acceptance

Knowing yourself means having a deep understanding of your personality, values, beliefs, strengths, weaknesses and emotions. It involves being self-aware and recognizing how your thoughts and actions impact your life and the lives of those around you. When you know yourself, you are better able to make decisions that align with your goals and values and you are more confident in your ability to navigate challenges and pursue personal growth. Ultimately, knowing yourself is important for developing a sense of purpose and fulfilment in life.

My journey of getting to know myself started in 2007 when I moved back to Melbourne having lived in Queensland for seven years. In 2008, I was hairdressing from home and through a client I met an amazing medium who, in turn, introduced me to my first spiritual mentor. This was the first step of my journey.

One of the first things that fascinated me was coming to understand that we all view the world through our own filters of experiences, beliefs, upbringing, fears, traumas, past hurts and more. These filters determine how we view the world, ourselves and others.

It was through this learning that it became easier for me to accept others for who they were and have compassion for their actions and reactions. I didn't necessarily agree or like them – I had a better level of acceptance and understanding for their behaviours.

It's interesting observing how people place expectations onto others – to assume and want others to act as they would.

We all do it. It's also interesting to notice the upset and frustrations they express when people don't do as they would like them to.

That was me. I still catch myself expecting other people to act as I would, before reminding myself - they are not me.

They have their own filters and experiences that are not mine.

Again, I don't have to like it, or agree. Instead, accept them where they are at.

This enables me to step back, remove any 'hooks' and release any emotional charge that ruffles my inner calm.

Everyone is on their own journey. Our power lies in how we choose to respond.

Knowing myself meant meeting parts of myself that I didn't or don't like. I would often avoid looking at these parts in the past. It can be confronting! However, these are parts of us that, when we do meet them, have the potential to teach us – if we are willing to look and get curious.

Meeting my ego and knowing how to use it as a tool in my self-discovery, was a game changer. It is also something I share with my clients.

Changing the narrative around the ego is a mission of mine, to understand that "ego" has a purpose. It helps to keep you alive. When you shove it aside and reject it - you are rejecting an aspect of yourself. The ego is a small part of you. It's not your whole identity.

Ego dislikes being challenged, criticised and change!

I encourage you to be mindful of your inner chatter, your Ego will keep you small, your Higher-Self will be encouraging you to grow in a healthy and expansive way.

2. Like your self - confidence

We need to meet ourselves where we are. Liking yourself means having a positive self- image and feeling good about who you are. It involves accepting your strengths and weaknesses, treating yourself with kindness and respect and recognizing your own value and worth. When you like yourself, you are more confident and resilient and better able to navigate life's challenges.

How do you show yourself that you like yourself?

You have this divine vessel – your human body – that allows you to experience life through all of your senses. Touch, taste, hear, see, smell.

It's always working, it's always there for you - injured or not. The body is the anchor for your soul and I believe the soul's purpose is to experience life and all it has to offer. The good, the bad, the ugly and the glorious.

This is not about standing naked in front of the mirror and loving what you see: Yet.

Start small. What is something about your Self that you are grateful for?

It is easy to like the good parts of your Self. The game changer for me was to like ALL aspects of myself.

I used to challenge my Self and let go of something for the year. For example; meat, sugar, alcohol etc. One year I gave up makeup. This was in the pursuit of learning to like myself. It was about putting away the mascara and eyeliner so I could meet the real me. The human version of me rather than the made-up me.

It was important for me to help myself overcome the pressure and comparisons of the media narrative of "not being enough".

And, honestly, this is an ongoing journey for me. I have found though, that I can now always find something – no matter how small it seems – to be grateful for in my Self.

3. Trust your self – soverence

Trusting yourself means having confidence in your abilities, decisions, and judgment. It involves listening to your inner voice and being true to your values and beliefs. When you trust yourself, you can make choices that align with your goals and aspirations; even in the face of uncertainty or adversity. It also means acknowledging your limitations and being willing to learn and grow from your experiences. Ultimately, trusting yourself is an important aspect of building self-esteem and experiencing fulfilment.

As you practice the first two foundational lessons, the more trust falls into place. When you know your triggers, current values, beliefs, your EGO; the natural by-product is TRUST. You can practise this by starting to take notice of any messages of wisdom that drop in to Your head – like; "Take the umbrella"; "Turn left; "Introduce yourself to them".

Start to get curious and have fun with it! You may not get it 'right' all the time, that's ok! Start connecting with your body and learn how it responds to different contexts. Tap into YOU.

For a long time, I had a niggle to introduce massage into my Reiki & Seichim business. Time and time again, I ignored it, simply because other people dissuaded me – and I chose to listen to them.

I was told to "stick with one thing", "you don't need to add anything else", and "what you are doing is enough". This was during the time I was learning to find my way forward in a relationship and situation that was less than fulfilling.

Once I removed myself from my marriage, the niggle returned. I was drawn to Lomi Lomi massage - a beautiful Hawaiian technique that has a spiritual foundation which would enhance the energy work I was already doing.

Once again, I tested the opinions of others and was again discouraged. My dad liked it but suggested, "to be safe, just do 'normal' massage".

This time, instead of choosing to listen to others, I listened to me.

My self-awareness practices kicking in!

I followed my instinct and completed my certification in Lomi Lomi massage. As a result, I developed my Divine Nurturing Package and my business grew into a gorgeous practice that financially supported me and my children. How nourishing!

Trusting myself and taking the plunge to follow my instinct, not only allowed for expansion in my business – but also in my Self. And the more I practiced trusting myself, the easier it became.

Now me in 2023 – life has been great and it's been terrible. It's been challenging and expansive. And through it all, I am owning who I am. I have boundaries that can be flexible. I have learnt to befriend parts of me that I don't necessarily like and I continue to explore my own Self on my Self-Mastery journey.

I still want to throw the towel in sometimes! I can have tantrums, and I still love the journey! My mission is to continue to check in on myself.

Keep what is working, tweak what needs tweaking and discard the outdated. To continue to Know, Like and Trust myself on every part of the journey.

I know who I am becoming. I like who I am becoming and I trust myself in the process. I am delivering to the best of my ability and meeting myself where I am, every day.

We are always changing. Give yourself permission to change.

My soul was craving peace, expansion and freedom. What does yours want? The world needs more happy humans.

As a Self-Mastery Coach, it's my passion to remind my clients it is not about being 'perfect' or having your shit together all the time.

It's about empowering your Self by bringing awareness to your Self; taking responsibility for our choices, actions and reactions.

Self-mastery is conscious living and honest self-reflection. Meeting your Self where you are at each moment. Getting through one day at a time. Taking the learnings and feedback from the previous day to be better, do better and move forward in your life in a way you feel proud and peaceful. Self-mastery is being witness to all aspects of your Self - the good, bad and the ugly!

It's an opportunity for you to stand in your power and work on your ability to control your thoughts, emotions, and behaviours so you can achieve your personal goals and lead a fulfilling life. It involves developing a strong sense of self-awareness, self-discipline, and self-control through intentionally tapping into yourself.

It is a lifelong journey, one that requires patience and self-commitment which will expand you and help nourish your soul. And you don't have to do it on your own.

What would it feel like if you Knew, Liked and Trusted yourself?

When you build a glorious relationship with yourself by connecting with and exploring deeper into all aspects of Self – your life will look, be and feel different. It changes your outlook, your actions, your reactions, your perception of the world and how you interact in it.

Are you ready for Glorious?

About the Author

Emily Pettigrew works as a Self-Mastery Coach, Teacher/Trainer, and Natural Energy Practitioner, on the Mornington Peninsula, Victoria. She is a qualified Reiki & Seichim Master and Teacher and shares her tried and tested strategies with those who are seeking to step back into the person they know they are and want to be, to feel strong and own their life again after feeling lost, empty and unfulfilled. She is passionate about reminding her clients it is not about being 'perfect', the Self Mastery path is about empowering your Self by bringing awareness to your Self; taking responsibility for your choices, actions and reactions.

Emily helps women through her Coaching/Mentoring, workshops, teaching, Women's Circles and 'on the table' healing services.

Website: www.emilypettigrew.com.au
Email: divineenergyalchemy@gmail.com
Facebook: www.facebook.com/emily.pettigrew.75

Sharyn Powlesland

I had a pretty normal childhood and teenage years – whatever normal is. By normal, I mean 2 parents and a sibling; a father who worked and a mother who ran their business and looked after the household and children, in a small country town.

We had chores. We walked a mile to school, and back every school day. Every year in the Christmas school holidays, for the whole of January, we went on our annual holidays. Dad's work van was refitted with mattresses and cupboards and we went travelling and camping. We camped on river banks and in National parks, from the Snowy Mountains to the Victorian High Country, the Grampians to Wilson's Promontory, and the western Victorian beaches, catching our own food – rabbits, fish and the occasional duck. As we grew older and too big for the van, a holiday house was let, and we explored the areas surrounding. Most years were somewhere different, but occasionally we'd revisit a previously loved area, or an area that we hadn't thoroughly explored the first time…

As I turned thirteen, we moved from our little wooden house to a new brick house my parents had designed and built in another part of our town. Dammit, I still had to share a bedroom with my sister! I mean seriously, surely some privacy was in order now that we were teens? But no, in fact our new bedroom was markedly smaller than the old one. In contrast, our lounge room was enormous. My parents were very happy and satisfied with their new house though. It had a designated office, and a very large shed for Dad's side of the business. Dad worked long hours; his business was dependent upon the dairy industry and this was ruled by the time's cows were milked. He tried to be home for meals and some family time at night, although, there were many times he wasn't home due to a breakdown or emergency.. I've come to believe that this was his way of avoiding our teen years, Mum's early onset menopause and the emotional issues this combination created. I, too, spent a lot of time, esp weekends out on the family farm. My sister spent time with other friends and boyfriends.

It was at this time that Mum fell from her pedestal, for me. I realised her hypocrisy, her quiet passive-aggressive abuse of Dad, and ultimately us girls - this had a profound effect.. I left home as soon as I'd finished High School at 17. Mum refused me going on to Year 12 because they "couldn't afford for both my sister and I to go on". Neither of us completely finished High School. I wanted to go to University. No money for that.. .yet Mum would spend money on cigarettes, spirits (not ghosts) and clothes. Not designer, expensive clothes, but cheap discounted things like tracksuits and t-shirts of which she'd buy multiples in one shop. When she died we found wardrobes of new, unworn clothes, and bottle of spirits secreted away in unexpected, as well as the usual places. Dad announced that he "could start a sly grog shop" with all that he'd found as he cleaned out cupboards and assessed his life in the months after Mum's death.

I left home with a group of friends, one of whom was my boyfriend of two years. We found a flat and jobs very easily. One became a Cop, another two became public servants, and I tried a variety of jobs as I started to discover adult life and it's responsibilities, and it's freedoms.

For the most part we didn't take life too seriously. It was rare for us all to be home at the same time, but we did try to have dinner together every Thursday (payday) at the local pub.

Things began to unravel when my boyfriend came home from a few days away and announced, very casually, after we had made love, "Oh by the way, I fucked J while I was there. Don't worry, it was nothing. Just thought I should let you know."

Ugh......at 18, how do you handle this, from the man you thought you could trust your life with?

I did the worst thing possible, I went and did the same thing with one of our neighbours….then told my lover. No moral high ground here. D'oh, what was I thinking? Not to mention the neighbour was much older and came before he went…

Things began to quietly go downhill after that. After one particularly awful physical incident and fight, I left and went to stay with a cousin, some suburbs away. As house space was limited, it was decided that I would sleep on a spare mattress on my cousin's marital bedroom floor for that night. That only lasted the one night, as my cousin's husband decided that I was fair game and that he'd get into bed with me and get lucky. My cousin had taken sleeping pills, so her hubby thought, and would be out of it all night, he told me. I fought him and yelled enough for him to get off me and go back to his own bed, but sleep was not happening for me from then on, until he went to work in the early hours. My cousin had called my boyfriend, and to this day I still don't know how she got his number or even knew who he was.

Once more into the frying pan, but I knew I couldn't keep going in this situation and was working to save some money to get out on my own. Footnoot: my boyfriend did actually end up married to J, not for long though; and they had a child.

Then along came John. Met at work. A lovely, almost innocent-seeming man with a quiet caring manner. We dated quietly, we thought, until an Italian workmate announced her claim to John, and punched me in the nose, enough to knock me out and cause black eyes for a week. In hindsight, I should have walked away from it all. I did, but he walked with me and took me to board with his sister, until I could find somewhere else.

We ended up living together, conveniently. For the most part things were good, I thought.

I had been working as a Motor Mechanic Apprentice, but that fell in a hole through no fault of mine. Finding it was very difficult for a woman to find work in a male dominated area, and being unemployed for several months led me to sit the Public Service exam and be offered a position in a local office. This gave me a sense of security and set me up in my mother's esteem.

But things weren't all a bed of roses, and I was beginning to find myself on the end of a fist, leaving a body-print in the wall, and being belittled verbally. The Pollyanna in me wanted to believe the best, and that I had somehow contributed to any given situation because I was working and he wasn't. The most common complaint of his. In one two year period he had 26 different jobs.

In our second year together he "went away for work" for a short time. I now know that is code for a short stay courtesy of Her Majesty. I was so dependant upon him that I "missed" him terribly and when he came home we became engaged, with plans to marry the following year or two. Meanwhile, my parents were planning a trip around Australia, and my mother had decided that we would be good candidates as house-sitters, esp as neither of us was working - at the time of her decision. BUT....we would need to be married, it being a country town and all, and well there was my parent's reputation to think of. It would be a new start, together, with the support of a country town, yadda yadda yadda. We acquiesced and agreed to be married, to his delight and my growing fears.

The week before we were to be married I was offered the Public Service job, and without thinking, accepted it. We were to be married on the 19th, I was to start work on the 21st and had booked for my licence on the 24th. I achieved all three; lasted 4 years in the marriage, 20 years in the public service and I still have my car licence. Needless to say, we didn't house-sit for my parents; the job being far too precious to my mother for me to give it up. The wedding could not be cancelled, according to my mother, as she would lose money, grog, and face. I was terrified, knowing I was making the biggest mistake of my life, and not being able to express it in words that anyone, even my best friend, would hear.

Eleven months later we were involved in a very serious head-on car accident. My husband was driving, under the influence of alcohol, and no one in the car was game say anything, especially after our friend offered to drive and was told quite strongly that he "was fine to drive". None of us had any other way of getting home that night, as it was late and we were over an hour from home.

My husband had severe lacerations to his head where he had hit the windscreen, the other two people had minor bumps and bruises, being in the backseat. I, on the other hand, suffered a full body whiplash which damaged vertebrae in my spine and paralysed me from the waist down. I was in excruciating pain that felt like I was sitting on the bloody stump of my torso, with no sensation from there down.

I realised then, that I had "known" that if I ever had a serious car accident that I would be paralysed, from the time I was about 12. At that moment I was relieved and released from that premonition, and determined to see this as a positive. I would walk again!

At the time, my parents were travelling to Australia for the second time, and were uncontactable – no mobile phones, sat navs, etc 40 years ago, so the hospital was relying on the Police. It took more than five days to find them, that by pure chance, and another nine days for them to make their way back to Victoria from somewhere remote in Western Australia.

Exactly three months later, on Australia Day, I walked out of the hospital Spinal Unit, albeit with a splint on one leg and two forearm crutches. But I walked! Scary and euphoric describes how I felt. I went on to two years of intensive physiotherapy, and returned to work a year after the accident, while still undergoing physio.

Three years later I bore my first child, a son. This was something that I was advised may never happen. While pregnant, I bought my first home, from money I had saved prior to my marriage and the accident. While in the later vulnerable stages of pregnancy I was "bullied" into adding my husband to the title. A year later, I separated my husband from our home, but not our lives.

The next 10 years were a mix of happiness and fear, as he stalked me, lied to me, tried to run me and our child off the road on an overpass, went to jail several times, broke into my house until I sold it and moved. My happiness came from several relationships and the support of friends and workmates through it all. Every Family Court case I attended, for either child support or access in the previous 10 years, I lost to him. Finally, at the 10-year mark, he sealed his own fate by threatening the life of a Registrar and also my Lawyer on the same day. He'd already been threatening my life many times since separation, but this all fell on deaf ears at the Family Court. All previous orders against me were withdrawn, my requests for child support and DVO were recognised, and I was advised to leave the area, even the State.

I went into hiding immediately, leaving my home and all my animals to be cared for by friends. Within six months, I had moved 3000kms away to start a new life with my new partner, soon to become husband, and my son. This was a good, but very broke time of my life. We soon had a brother for my son, a little farm, and a very caring community.

My husband was a decent bloke, all things considered, hedonistic but kind and generous. Until I discovered he couldn't keep his dick in his pants. I gave him six months grace to determine where his priorities lay, as he was working away for a month at a time, with a week home, which didn't really give us much time to spend together. His priorities proved to be with himself and not his family, so we separated—on reasonable terms.

Four years later, I met my last partner. Although we didn't marry, I considered us committed, especially when we bought a property together and had a daughter he wasn't meant to be able to father. A low sperm count and 55 years of age with no previous children. I had jokingly said "if anyone can get pregnant, it's me" and promptly did.

This was the most insidious and masked abusive relationship due to the abuse being emotional and financial, mainly. He demanded that all my money from my property sale go into our new property; I kept $20,000 hidden in an investment account. He wanted me to add my super from my Govt job to his Super, which I declined much to his disgust. He demanded all joint accounts; I only agreed to the mortgage and an offset account, keeping my accounts separate, again to his chagrin. He would demand to know where I'd been if I went to the shops and wasn't back when he expected me to be, despite my having phoned him while out to see if he wanted anything. I was accused of going out for lunch with my girlfriend as a cover for meeting my lover. Who has the time or energy for that when you have three children, a house and an insecure partner to take care of? Although my oldest had left home by this time, we had my partner's stepdaughter (his ex-wife's daughter) living with us, which was fraught on its own.

Most of the time, his stepdaughter and I got along reasonably well – especially when it was girl-talk. Yet, as soon as he would come home the energy would change, and he had to be the focus of everyone's attention (as did she when he was around).

One afternoon as she and I were sitting at the kitchen table just idly chatting about life, the Universe and everything, he came home and on feeling our bonhomie, had to disrupt. Rather than enjoy the fact we were getting along so well, he chose to play us off, emotionally, against each other. I sensed myself participating in a way reminiscent of my 15 year old self at home with my younger sister (the stepdaughter was the same age, 13), and he, our mother. I remember thinking to myself "Hey, I'm the adult here. Stop this, Sharyn!" but I couldn't help but be drawn into the bickering that was happening. Suddenly, it dawned on me exactly what was happening, I quickly stepped out the door, away from it all. I found myself banging my head against the verandah post, thinking "I've married my mother! Oh, help!"

It was in that moment that the little ember under the log that I'd become, flared up and said "Enough!" This stops here unless you want your daughter, or even step-daughter to be in the exact same type of relationship, to see that this is OK, and even think it's 'normal'.

In that moment I knew I had to end the relationship……but how? It was evidently too good to leave in the eyes of any observer), but getting too bad to stay, for me.

It took another two years, of worsening insecurities on his part, and building of courage on mine. It was an incident that began rather pettily, but the words he used tore my heart out and trampled it, changing everything.

In desperation to get the upper hand, he vehemently spat at me, "I can understand why your first husband raped you…and beat you!" I stood stock still, in shock. Shocked that someone who professed love, and supposedly cared about me, could use that information against me; it had been disclosed in confidence for him to better understand me. A million thoughts ran through my head, not least of all, "What!? You can understand?? Does this mean you would do that as well?" I hauled my arm back and slapped him hard. As he cowered over the bench, complaining/whining that I had assaulted him and he could have me charged, I punched him in the arm repeatedly, and then told him to get out, we are done! He did leave eventually a few weeks later, when he realised that my continued sleeping in our daughter's room wasn't going to change, and went to live in our converted shed. Temporarily, for three whole years! He moved and remarried 14 years ago.

What I've learned, and shown myself, is that I am stronger than I ever thought. I have courage I didn't know I had. Resilience that has kept me alive. I've come back from paralysis, not once, but twice in my life. Yes, I walk, albeit slower and more carefully now.

I've survived two abusive relationships, well actually three, when you count my mother, who taught me to accept abuse.

I have survived! I am living a good life. You can too. Take one day at a time and Look forward.

About the Author

I'm a mother two sons and a daughter. Sole parent for most of their lives. Grandmother to two beautiful boys. Survivor of spinal paralysis, twice, 40 years apart. Survivor of relationship abuse three times—my mother, and two male partners. I'm a mother, a lover, a grandmother and survivor.

I've worked in a diverse variety of employment. I've been an actor with an Amateur theatre group, with the opportunity to Direct and Produce plays, as well as assist with costuming and sets. Loved my time there!

I love horses and cats; and my children and grandchildren, of course! I've travelled Australia, as well as Thailand and New Zealand. I'd do it all again!

Facebook: www.facebook.com/sharyn.powlesland/
Email: wildbrumby58@yahoo.com.au

Alyson Richelle Ray

Have you ever felt different, awkward, and/or alone but never understood why?

Do you often question events in your life and ask why me?

I am here to let you know that you aren't alone. You might be different. We are all different. There is nothing wrong with being different.

You are perfect! Exactly the way you are supposed to be.

I'm here to help you embrace being different, find your true self, your purpose and unconditional love for yourself.

Sharing my journey is something many suggested. To them I've been an inspiration. I'd questioned whether I had anything worthwhile to share.

I've always wanted to make an impact, change lives, and make a difference. Helping you embrace everything you are. All your quirks and unique gifts that make you, rather than believing there is something wrong.

I'm hoping that I can help you find your voice and be a voice for those that need it. I'm hoping to inspire you to find your purpose, so that you can live your best life, doing what you love.

Letting you know that it's okay to be different and do things others may not agree with. This is YOUR LIFE.

Do what you are destined to do! I want you to follow your dreams and passions. I'm your cheerleader helping you make it happen.

Life is an adventure and journey. We need to accept and appreciate our past, as without our past, we wouldn't be here today.

If I didn't have my past, I wouldn't be here now.

I am so grateful for my past.

It was a journey to help find my inner strength. What is important and what I value. You can have all this too.

I'm here to help and support you. If you choose, we all have a choice. We can choose positive or negative. Everything can be positive. If we choose it, choose to see the positives and live your best life.

We all have a starting point.

I was born in a small country town, out of wedlock to parents that were no longer together. My father didn't know I was on the way. Another man was with my mother and wanted to be my father. I was given up for adoption so that a couple could raise me.

I was initially fostered by an amazing couple, Beryl and Richie and their daughters. My eldest son Thomas is named after them and my middle name, Richelle is in recognition of Richie. A lifelong relationship formed with the Thomas family. It's a pleasure and honour to be included by this family. Without them my life wouldn't be what it is today.

Mum and Dad collected me and raised me as their own. They always told me I was unique and wanted. They were unable to have a child of their own. Adopting me made their dreams of becoming parents a reality.

I remember growing up and feeling like I was different and an outsider. I didn't find it easy to make friends. I often spent time alone, not having many friends.

I started working from a young age and did two jobs during my final year at school to keep myself busy, gaining independence and freedom.

A conversation at the Royal Easter Show had me apply to the NSW Police.

I was accepted, just days after receiving my HSC results. A new chapter began. Leaving home for the first time and having to do things myself. Lots of training and study. Making new friends and surviving in an environment which was foreign.

Joining the NSW Police at 19 was eye opening and a life changing experience. 15 years of service, reaching the rank of Senior Sergeant, ended with a medical discharge. A huge adjustment and learning about Complex Post Traumatic Stress Disorder (CPTSD) and the way it impacts your life, your relationships and sense of self.

Living with CPTSD is a daily challenge. It wreaked havoc on my relationship, my children and my family. Friends and family struggled with the emotional roller coaster I was experiencing. Trying to juggle appointments, young children and trying to understand triggers. I hit breaking point. I couldn't cope any more or look after myself or my family.

I needed more help than I was getting from medication, regular psychologists, and psychiatrist appointments. I was struggling to deal with surveillance from the insurance company, constant questions and having to jump through hoops. Nightmares, hypervigilance, the panic attacks were some of the daily struggles.

Needing more help, we sought help from family and moved again. This move caused a great divide. It was also a memorable experience to live with Nan, who cared and supported us at a time of need.

From Nan's place, I went and did a 21-day mental health inpatient program at St John of God. A time to just focus on myself, my health and getting better. Getting to know the ins and outs of CPTSD. Understanding my triggers and coping strategies. Finding healthier ways to cope and manage.

Being around others with CPTSD was refreshing and freeing. I didn't feel alone. I didn't feel like there was something wrong. I felt accepted and understood. I learnt that I needed to accept and appreciate myself.

I realised that I needed to put myself first and look after me. Without putting on my oxygen mask or having a full tank I couldn't provide and care for those I loved. I couldn't provide and care for my family.

How often do you look after you first?

Do you take time out to refuel your tank and care for your needs?

You aren't being selfish. You're being a role model, teaching those around you the importance of self-care and looking after themselves.

Being a mum was always something I had dreamed about. My early 20s I was diagnosed with endometriosis and Polycystic Ovarian Syndrome (PCOS). I was shattered by this Doctor telling me I would never be able to have children.

Years later I realised the impacts of these diagnoses on my fertility and dreams. An ectopic pregnancy misdiagnosed from 6 weeks gestation on multiple occasions as just severe morning sickness, ruptured weeks late. I was rushed to the main hospital from my local hospital.

I was critical and bleeding internally.

I'm grateful for medical technology. It saved my life, allowing me to share this with you.

Months later just before Christmas I experienced similar symptoms. Off to Emergency, before being transferred to the main hospital. Again, another ectopic pregnancy around 9 weeks gestation.

The Dr told me that IVF would be successful as I was highly fertile. I didn't want to hear this. I felt like I drew the short straw and learnt I didn't like statistics.

I was grieving. Why me? Why did falling pregnant have to be so hard. All I wanted was to be a Mum.

IVF was successful the first time. Thomas joined our family, making me a Mum. Madison was a journey.

Nanna passed away during our first frozen transfer which was an early miscarriage.

Overstimulation from the fresh IVF cycle with 13 embryos collected. I felt like I was constantly being poked and prodded as a guinea pig. Multiple early miscarriages again.

On our 5th attempt, Mum offered to assist and paid our out-of-pocket expenses from Nanna's Wil.

A close friend was doing her first IVF cycle at the same time. She shared that her cycle was negative. Just days later I found out my cycle was a success, and I was pregnant. It was heartbreaking having to share our news, knowing that my friend was grieving.

Around 20 weeks, we found out that another close friend had to deliver their little princess. This little princess had grown her wings. Always remembered and missed by her family and brothers.

It was such a difficult time. I was carrying my little girl, whilst they had to say farewell and goodbye to their little girl. I will never forget you princess or being told of your passing.

Madison was in a hurry to enter the world. An emergency c-section after she went into distress, having meconium in her waters. Reflecting afterwards on prior weeks, early labour and contracts had caused issues. I should have paid more attention. I'm lucky my little girl was okay.

Falling pregnant, pregnancy and labour was not easy. I did things differently and felt alone. Why couldn't I just do it like others?

I saw so many around me constantly pregnant, having children and them placed into care. Many friends struggled to make their dreams of becoming parents a reality. I often questioned why? Why do some just fall pregnant so easily, whilst those that desperately want to be parents' struggle. How is that fair? Unfortunately, it's all part of the journey.

The birth of Thomas and Madison had me asking more questions about myself and genetics. Finding and meeting my mother and father was a huge part of my finding and understanding myself. I felt like I belonged and was part of something.

Being diagnosed with Autism Spectrum Disorder (ASD) and Attention Deficit Hyperactive Disorder (Inattentive) (ADHD-

Inattentive) were huge milestones. My children have an ASD diagnosis. To me, a diagnosis was an eye opener. A way to help get more assistance and be understood. A way to understand yourself and why.

Finding I was like my children allowed me to be more accepting and understanding. I now understood why I struggled with many things yet succeeded with so many others. Without knowing the truth and reason we can often be critical and judgemental. Many don't like labels.

The labels as many like to call them, were life changing. They allowed me to be able to move forward, accepting my strengths and weaknesses. I accepted and understood myself.

Growing up I loved to do jigsaw puzzles. I would say that my life felt very much like a jigsaw. I wanted to find and gather all the pieces that made me.

Our lives are multiple pieces of everything that happens. Let's put all your pieces together so that you can see the amazing individual you are. You are so strong and amazing. There is just one of you. Be proud and love everything that you are.

Many times, in my life I choose my own path, my own adventure. I fought for the underdog. I stood firmly on the things I believed and valued. Finding my voice happened many times over the years. Standing up and doing what I wanted and what was best for me. It caused tension and division. It caused me to be an outcast and targeted by others, who didn't believe in what I was doing.

Choices were made that weren't accepted or liked by others. I chose what I needed for myself and my family. This was difficult as I really wanted to fit in and be liked. Doing what others wanted wasn't of service to me, my life, and dreams. Sometimes we need to break the chains and do what is in our best interests. Living the life we desire. Having the life we want; rather than what others think we should have or want for us. It wasn't easy going against what others thought.

Would I do it again? Most definitely. Would I change the way I, did it? I would come from a greater place of understanding and compassion. I would really explain my needs and appreciation for what was being offered.

Have you ever found yourself moving or changing something, thinking that things would be different?

Moving became a habit. Moving workplaces and homes became a way to escape the past and start fresh. Unfortunately, the past always followed. It didn't always happen straight away, but eventually it caught up.

Moving to Queensland was a big change. It helped remove many triggers and issues. Unfortunately, many of the issues were inside, so they came with me. It just took many years to realise that everything in the past was inside me, and I needed to work on myself and be responsible. I couldn't keep running.

I have always wanted to create a more independent and better future for my family. I entered the workforce doing seasonal work. No support from the insurance company. All from my own desire to be free. This allowed me to find myself and that I was more than just a wife and mother.

I wanted more, so I started with Thermomix. I found I was able to help others and make a difference. I found my passion, inspiring and showing others how they can gain independence and live a better life doing things many take for granted.

I was here to serve, support and encourage. I used my differences to show others that there is nothing wrong with them and how to live their best life.

Having others inspired by my journey, my strengths, my passion and wanting to be guided and supported by me, helped me find my worth, purpose and passion.

I spent lots of time on a personal self-development journey, reflecting and exploring courses to help me identify my strengths. It helped me fight for what I want and to make a difference in my life and help others live their best life. I completed my Masters in Neurologist Programming (NLP) so that I could really help others transform the past so they could live their best life.

Separation, becoming an independent mum of three neurodivergent children (those that are different and have disabilities) and learning that during my relationship, there was domestic violence changed me. I had to accept my role and actions in everything. No one person can be blamed for anything. We all have a part to play.

I had to own my actions, my thoughts and the things that happened. I spent many days reflecting and thinking back on my life, the patterns, the behaviours, and the results.

I wanted to ensure that I stopped the patterns and gave my children a better life. I was responsible. I could change and make things better.

Standing up and accepting my role was necessary. We all make mistakes. We need to be able to forgive those and ourselves. We do our best in that moment with what we know. I learnt that it was okay to seek help and support from professionals. I needed to learn and understand what had happened.

Everything that has happened has helped me connect and inspire others to take a leap to create more. I've been able to guide and encourage a Mother to step outside her comfort zone, leaving a job where she wasn't valued, into something where she now shines and motivates others. Taking a leap of faith, knowing that there was so much potential and change. Believing that she wasn't alone and would be supported. Now a valued team member honouring herself, her skills and commitment to brighten others life. Making a difference and helping others live their best lives.

I know how hard it can be when you're feeling overwhelmed, frustrated. Thinking you don't fit in and aren't understood by those around you. I want to help you understand yourself and how everything fits perfectly together. I want to see you shine and live your best life.

You don't need to prove yourself to anyone. You are amazing and need to see and believe it. Everything you need and have ever needed is inside you. You are valuable and wanted. Let's uncover your authentic self so that you can shine, live your life on purpose with passion. I want you to be a role model and shining star, to those around you.

Much of my life I didn't fit in and didn't understand why. Did I make my life more difficult? Most likely. Have you felt like you haven't fit in and have done things differently trying to find your tribe and where you fit. I want to help you find the passion in your belly so you can shine. We need to work together, to inspire each other, to be the best versions of ourselves, the best at everything that we do.

My life and journey have brought me here to help you. I really want to be able to help. I can help create the life of your dreams, so that we can go on and cause a rippled effect. We are all here to help each other. To be inspired, encouraged, and grow. Don't hold yourself back. Now's your time to shine.

Now is your time, just like it is mine, to find where you fit. To find where you belong and those that are just like you. You aren't alone. You have a tribe that wants to include and accept you. It all starts with you.

My goal is to work with Mums who are ready and want to find themselves, completing the jigsaw puzzle. It doesn't matter if your journey is different to mine. I want to work with those to help them find themselves and find their passion. You don't need to be experiencing domestic violence or neurodivergent. You just need to believe and want to be the shining star.

Live your best life with no regrets, doing the things that you want to do. Helping you achieve your dreams, believing in yourself, and more importantly accepting, because when we accept ourselves, we make a difference.

You can create your own circle, your own family. That's who you need to be around. You deserve to be surrounded by love and accepted. It's okay to say no if people don't accept you and don't treat you appropriately. I know how hard it can be to stand up to those who treat you poorly, don't respect you or your boundaries.

Go out and find your tribe. Find those that accept and love you for who you are.

I see you.

I support you.

I want you to thrive and live your best life.

About the Author

Alyson is a mother of three young children. She created Embracing Different and Build Independence and Skills to empower and change the lives of others in the community. She is passionate about increasing independence, inclusion and provides a welcoming space for everyone to enjoy, where they can play, meet animals, and connect with others.

She empowers and inspires others to find themselves and break through barriers to live their best life using a variety of techniques. She is always looking for ways to grow personally, as well as to boost others, to be a great cheerleader and mentor.

She loves jigsaw puzzles, Lego and travelling. Exploring new places and making memories with family and friends is important.

Email: alysonrichelle@proton.me
Facebook: www.facebook.com/nosyla
Linktr.ee: https://linktr.ee/AlysonRay

Liz Rotherham

'You can bounce back too'

Well, it's been 4 years since my last book and whew what a different rollercoaster of a life that has been and where has the time gone! I am sitting here now running my own mental health and wellbeing charity which has always been a passion of mine and think to myself how did I get here?

I used to feel like a fly in a spider's web just stuck and not able to free myself. Tangled in an emotional bubble of life's challenges and not truly being me. I lived behind a mask for years!

Personally, the past is the past and this chapter is not about dwelling on matters gone by. It's important to know however, that life has not been easy, and I have spent years reliving the fears and extreme challenges, which I am not keen on doing again. If you are interested to hear more about my story of living with Bipolar and from a different perspective, then grab a copy of my book "Life as a Rollercoaster" from Amazon or my website www.heads2minds.co.uk.

I will, however, give a little reflection as this helps put things in perspective. I do question why did I live in a bubble for so long, why did I pretend that everything was ok? The mask I hid behind is now well and truly removed! Perhaps it's when you hit 50 that you frankly stop worrying what people think and just be yourself. When we start growing up, it's like we have signed up to the 18-40-60 and I quote "when you are 18 you worry about what everybody is thinking of you." I can vouch for that; my gorgeous nieces do all the time. "When you are 40, you don't give a darn what anybody thinks of you and when you are 60 you realise nobody's been thinking about you at all."

I can honestly say I have never been happier; I still have challenges but am in a better mind set and am able to deal with life! By the way, what on earth is currently happening in the world?

I tend to avoid the news and don't read the newspapers; however, people relay information, and I can honestly say I think the world has lost the plot or at least some of it has! It's quite ironic when you don't watch the news that your mindset improves as the media do tend to portray news in a negative way.

Now, mental health has always been my passion, with a diagnosis of Bipolar and mainly psychosis. I have extremely good insight into my condition and have learnt what my triggers are and how to manage them. I describe myself as Tigger from Winnie the Pooh, Tigger bounces up and down with bundles of energy, however Tigger does have down days and so do I.

Voices of Impact

The other day I was jumping up and down in the CEO's office of Essex NHS Foundation Trust like an excited bunny! Thankfully, he was laughing! It's because I am so passionate about helping people and at long last people are listening and collaborating together to support each other. When we deliver workshops to Primary schools, Tigger (Teddy bear) joins me and helps educate and keep the children engaged. You have to be relatable otherwise children especially see through this! I normally introduce myself with having ADD or tendencies of ADHD. Some children put their hand up and tell me too! My response is join the club! We need to ensure that children don't feel like they are different or isolated because of this. We are all unique in our own skills, abilities and personality and I encourage to embrace this and be yourself. When I say this, I am not saying it is easy, far from it however why pretend to be something you are not as this I believe brings unhappiness and a feeling of being trapped.

Being open and honest is one of my highest values and beliefs, which sometimes gets me into trouble. Wild child for sure when I grew up, I spent numerous occasions on the naughty step at school. Do you remember in the amusement arcades a game with a toy hammer and you could bop all the animals that popped up. Well, that was me, every time someone told me off, I was back up again like a yoyo. Extremely wearing as my mother used to say! In fact, she still says it to me now at the grand old age of 52!

Now as you know my nickname is Tigger and Tigger likes

challenges, so, in my intimate wisdom my friend and I decided to go on silent retreat. I know what you are thinking, how can a lady whose nickname is Tigger go on that. Well, everybody who knows me said the same. 'There is no way you can do that'. Challenges or External parties doubting my ability, makes me want to do it more!! Not talking for 3 days! Walk in the park or so I thought!

I ended up having another episode, it wasn't psychosis as I know the difference, it was PTSD.

The venue was amazing it was an old castle in the middle of Wales, beautiful in fact and it reminded me of the castle out of Harry Potter! I presumed we would stay in the castle, but we were shown an area at the back which was several cottages with rooms. As soon as I saw it, I had an eery feeling, you know the one you get when you feel something is just not right. 9/10 times I trust my gut and my spider senses were heightened but I still went in.

As soon as the lady showed me my room, it took me right back to when I was sectioned in a Mental Hospital, the feeling was overwhelming, and it brought back all my worst nightmares. It was an exact replica of my room that I inhabited on numerous occasions. My first instinct was to pack up, but I thought about it and the need to face my fear and prove to others that I could be silent forced me on.

My friend and I were shown around the main castle and what were expected over the next couple of days, and she looked decidedly uneasy which was odd.

We sat in silence at the dinner which was a practice for what lay ahead over the next couple of days. My friend did not look happy, but I was ok.

At 8pm that night we were told that we were not allowed to speak until the end of the retreat. Bang silence! Walking back with my friend in silence was hard and we waved good night, I left and entered my room.

The fear hit me like a bolt of lightning, I took one look in the room and picked up all my bags and rushed outside. I thought I had the strength to do it but once again at night my fears came back. I hasten to add my friend and I scarpered and didn't look back! If you want the full story email me!! I also experienced the biggest panic attack in my life and was extremely thankful that my friend was there to calm me down.

I learnt a lot from that night, flashbacks, feeling of fear and panic and I sit now in reflection to understand why it happened and rationalise my behaviour, in order to help me grow in the future.

My PTSD lasted for a month when I got back and once again medication helped me calm down. Mum and my partner were fantastic and so were all the doctors. It was another massive learning curve and one that I now know how to recognise the difference in my mind between psychosis and PTSD. I have worked extremely hard over the years to understand my own mind as it is so powerful. Having the ability to manage your thoughts rather than let them overwhelm you is challenging. Mindfulness is a great tool for this.

I don't mean meditation although that can be part of the practice but building your mind muscle. Strengthening your brain muscle to help with overwhelming thoughts and the role plays that we often make up, like a hamster on a wheel.

I practice daily mindfulness. Like a physical body we have to keep our body active by movement. It is the same with the mind we need to be able to build our mind muscle and this can be done throughout the day with exercises that can strengthen this muscle. The more you practice the more your mind becomes stronger to allow you the ability to be able to control your thought process and have space to deal with daily life. Changing daily routines for example, brush your teeth with the opposite hand. Might sound bizarre but if you do this you are having to concentrate as it is out of character and feels different. Teaching you to bring your mind back to the present moment rather than automatic habits that keeps you in robot mode. I would highly recommend the book 'The Power of Now' this teaches you all about this, or practice changing patterns throughout your day.

I sometimes refer to myself as an upside-down swan! On the surface you see gracefulness and peace but under the water the swan's feet are paddling hard to swim. I choose the world to show Tigger, my energetic bubble of energy but my mind is calm on the inside although scatty on the outside!

Stopping drinking and smoking changed my life. It has been 7 years now! I used to be a huge binger drinker sometimes to the point I passed out due to drinking so heavily. Looking back, I was in denial and alcohol was also my coping mechanism along with biting all the skin around my nails until they hurt! I am now tee total and bouncing around like a space hopper! Sometimes it is hard to rain me in as I am so passionate about helping others and making a difference in this world. Using healthier coping strategies has made such a significant difference bringing clarity to my headspace.

I am not saying that I am now a transformed angel who doesn't experience any challenges far from it, but I know how to manage my emotions and reflect back on what I have learnt over the years. I still experience imposter syndrome; I think we all do at some point of our lives if we admit it. Belief in oneself and continual learning from others really helps. I am not the fount of all knowledge and nor do I think I am; however, I have helped many clients in many different ways.

I use different kind of techniques which is a combination of talking, hypnotherapy, mind coaching and energy management.

However, it depends on the client, empathy and trust is huge and feeling with that person really makes a difference. Both have a connection that feels comfortable otherwise it won't work.

If I let you into a secret, I used to do a lot of my meditation, mindfulness in a mental hospital for years, 20 in fact and then when I decided to leave the corporate world and concentrate on Self-care. My visualisation, planning goals and ideas started to happen. Thorough out my life whilst working I trained in lots of different modalities and am now fully qualified in many therapies and alternative healing. Clearing limiting beliefs and helping the client identify why they are feeling like they do, 9 times out of 10 stems from their childhood. Once you have identified the source you can heal by different methods in what the client is comfortable with. Talking, energy healing, mind coaching or journalling. Clients have left feeling much lighter and sometimes not sure how it happened. Like a weight has been lifted off their shoulders and they can breathe again.

For years people have thought I was completely bonkers however now, we have proof that what I have been practising does actually work. I discovered a book that was written by a lovely gentleman about 3 years ago called Why Woo Works! Hurrah!! I read it and thought thank you Dr Hamilton for explaining the science behind what I have been studying and experiencing for years.

It was like confirmation that I do know what I am talking about, and this helped with my confidence and ability to believe in myself.

I was introduced to a client about 6 years ago and I remember saying to him at the time, one day you will come to understand my world. He did say there is no way will you ever get me into woo woo land. He was ex-military and didn't want to open Pandora's box which I am not surprised considering some of the experiences he had to endure when serving. The majority of people only see it in films, but he had seen it first hand and relaying it to me as a therapist even I was emotionally affected. It is extremely hard to be on the receiving end of anyone's trauma or upsetting life experiences. We all have to have an outlet and take time out whether, physical, emotional or psychological hence why clinical supervision is so important.

We did some intense work and I hasten to add he is now understanding that perhaps we make sense and looking at the world from a different perspective. He has been one of my long-standing clients and now a friend in whom I confide, and he always offers me a different way of looking at the situation and vice versa. He is now well and truly in woo land! Lol!

He has more clarity now and can recognise triggers and knows how to deal with them. It's not easy and sometimes there is a wobble, but we are only human and there are still lessons to be learnt, it's what makes us stronger. If we shine a light and encourage people to find their own gift or superpower, accountability and ownership does help along with helpful strategies to support through everyday life.

I often say to people that we have the ability to time travel!! Not in the DeLorean in the 'Back to the Future' film but in our minds. You think about it, when we heard music that reminds us of a memory from the past or some-one talks about a scenario and then you are taken back they're in your mind. I say to people if it's a good memory then great as it creates feeling of warmth but if there is still bad feeling or negativity then perhaps it is time to face your fears and heal the past.

It is not easy and we in the charity encourage people to do this and provide a range of holistic therapies that are tailored to that individual.

It is quite surprising how many people put a mask up, the common saying is I'm fine, but this is not always the case. I used to use that just to not talk about how I really felt. Now I just show my emotion and vulnerability. I used to apologise and get embarrassed, now I embrace it as it is ok to show emotion and how are we ever going to change this world if we pretend to the world that everything is ok when it is sometimes not.

Heads2minds has only been going two years and already we have achieved and delivered some exciting projects! We are now working in partnership with the Essex NHS Trust, delivering Mental Health First aid in companies and schools, delivering

Emotional Wellbeing Programmes in Primary schools and just recently launched the Heads2minds Healing Heroes which each have gemstones and healing powers! Of course, we can't forget our adorable Pet therapy dogs, we currently have a team of 6 dogs who visit schools, care homes and hospitals and they do have gemstones and you can sponsor them. Heads2minds has also helped individual clients to and have 3 consultants that offer fantastic support to people.

Heads2minds charity values and beliefs are based upon authenticity, empathy and being genuine. Trust and honesty are also a big part of the charity. Accountability and also not being afraid to say you are in the wrong. I know we all have an EGO but it's good to tame that!

The heads2minds team deliver a variety of wellbeing training which involves people reflecting on their own life experiences and finding that perhaps they need to address situations that are uncomfortable in order to move forward. Sometimes it is not easy to face your past, fears or even demons but believe me once you do, your future path looks much clearer, and you are able to see the wood from the trees. Heads2minds has a wide network and blogs on specific subjects, so please reach out, if we can't help, we know someone who can.

Personally, I have found that sharing my lived experience is extremely powerful and can inspire people to dig deep and start healing. Talking at events, schools, corporate companies has helped not only on my journey but others to empower them to face their fears. I am like a phoenix and have that tattooed on my arm to represent that we can all rise from the ashes and live a healthy happier life once we acknowledge who we are, not be afraid to speak out, show some vulnerability and share our story. Once you do this, you will realise you are not alone.

With the right support, friends and family, anyone, like Tigger can bounce back too....

About the Author

Lizzie is extremely passionate about mental health and wellbeing and is the CEO of the charity Heads2minds which offers training, coaching, mentoring and holistic therapies for all people. Lizzie is a qualified clinical hypnotherapist, transformation coach and National Trainer. Skilled in NLP, Psychology, she has helped hundreds of people to find their voice, build confidence and lead happier healthier lives.

A self-published author and keynote speaker, Lizzie has won prestigious awards to recognise the work she provides within the health industry, featuring in the national and Local newspapers, she continues to encourage all to find their voice and speak their truth.

Lizzie loves to walk with her dogs in nature, singing in the shower and retreats, including travelling with her Mum!

Email: Liz@heads2minds.co.uk
Facebook, Instagram, TikTok: @Heads2minds
Website: www.heads2minds.co.uk

Danielle Simpson

Remove the masks to reveal your inner strength

I started my life as a miracle baby born eight weeks early by emergency caesarean weighing just 2lbs 4oz on my mother's nineteenth birthday in the Brisbane Mater Mothers Hospital, after her waters broke unexpectedly in the ambulance from Toowoomba.

Mum shared with me recently how scary the whole ordeal was and how hard it was to leave me and return home to Killarney, three hours away while I stayed in special care for five more weeks. They couldn't afford to stay in Brisbane and dad needed to work so they sent breast milk delivered by my nana in the truck or on the Greyhound coach daily that was tube fed to me by the nurses. Being the first grandchild, I was spoiled beyond measure and spent my first years with pops greasy hand prints on my white bonds singlets

Strength was ingrained in us from the start, and hard work was just the way of life. My nana would often say, "Hard work is in your blood", and so I learned from an early age where my strength came from and the value that everyone placed on it. In 1993, when I was just eight years old I was selected to train at Chandler in the Olympic gymnastics squad where I spent the next year practising each day after school. Even as a young girl, the training was intense, and the expectations were high. Even with bloodied and calloused hands I got back up with a smile on my face and kept going, there was no room for complaints or imperfection and you were expected to just suck it up and suck it in. I loved gymnastics and while it was a huge honour and opportunity, the treatment, trauma and the financial stress took away the fun, so I made the hard decision to quit and return to club gymnastics.

Growing Up

It felt like there was little choice but to be strong, raising my brother and baby sister after my mum and dad divorced, leaving me to support and help mum who uses a wheelchair to get around. There was no other option when it came to the school bullies. As the smallest kid in the grade, struggling with school and my ADHD, divorced parents, financial hardships and everyone knowing mum was in the chair, I had to put on a brave face if I was going to survive. School was tough and I spent a lot of time alone in the library with my head in books or in the school forest trying to escape my reality. Teachers had no idea how to help and when I wasn't hiding I was doing the only thing I felt I was good at, putting on a show and practising my gymnastics on the oval.

Into adulthood

I hid my diagnosis of ADHD and depression and was so scared of looking dumb, of failing and getting things wrong that I did everything I could to look normal. The pressure took its toll and resulted in many meltdowns and me leaving more jobs that I can count on one hand. I remember being in Bali in my room after a huge day of yoga teacher training in 2018, and suddenly recalling the day I quit the Olympic gymnastics training squad. I realised that I had held onto so much shame and feeling that I was a failure and had not even spoken about my time as a gymnast, not even with my closest friends. The decision to leave was the right one for me and my family and going back to dancing, tumbling, trampolining and being in my home club was much more fun but came with a good dose of disappointment from Dad. He put a lot of pressure on me and never really understood my challenges.

As an adult he criticised my choices and was often frustrated when I left a job, found something new and dove into my creative and curious side. It was hard to stay true to myself and exhausting as well, but I always held this hope in my heart that one day he and others would finally see me for who I was and I could stop trying to please and finally feel like I was loved and accepted just as I am.

In 2022 after the death of my dad

I spent months processing a lifetime of hopes, memories and for the most part an emotionally challenging and dysfunctional relationship. It was a difficult time with a lot of emotions coming up, but the one that surprised me the most was a feeling of relief, that he wouldn't be here to criticise me anymore and even more surprisingly was this feeling of grief, of losing that criticising voice. After all, it was all I knew and in many ways, what pushed me to try to do better. At the time, we were in the middle of the COVID saga and I was trying to decide if I was going to continue with my woodworking business or if I wanted to follow my true calling and start my business in yoga, coaching and Human Design to better support my own needs and others on their journey. It was a hard decision, but it felt like it had run its course and served its purpose. Probably the most profound lesson that came through was the unconscious unfolding of my lack of worthiness and a mindset piece that had me trying to prove myself yet again. This time I had created a hard-working job for myself, on the tools, using my hands and still desperately trying to seek my father's love and validation.

It was a huge realisation and a defining moment that stopped me in my tracks and helped me to heal and redirect that energy and an opportunity to redefine the concept of hard work, of strength and my own value and worth. I realised it didn't matter what anyone else thought, as long as I was happy and enjoying the process.

In hindsight, it was funny how he still didn't get it and was still constantly asking if I was selling anything or making any money, he struggled to believe those cute little wooden hair bows were a hit.

Dad wasn't an awful person. He wasn't exactly supportive of my choices and life, but I know now that his criticisms were from a place of love and wanting me and my siblings to have the best life we could. He didn't want us to struggle like he and mum had. I didn't know his parents or his family very well, but I got the impression they were similar to my grandparents, who respected hard work and a person's ability to dig deep and do whatever it took. I feel like he was trying to prove his worth to himself for his entire life. The sad thing was, he would often criticise himself and could never take a compliment. I just wish those conversations we loved and shared about science, space, music and movies could have formed a more balanced conversation and emotions and boundaries were seen as a strength instead of a weakness

Dad lost his job around 5 years ago due to a fall and not being able to work anymore. It saw his mental and physical health decline rapidly. He saw things in a very black and white way, you either had a job or you were looking for another one. I know it was really hard for him as he prided himself on being a hard worker and really it was his whole life and identity. Sadly he didn't really have any friends, but I was grateful that he made friends with two Persian cats that he lived with. They seemed to keep his spirits up and give him a reason to get out of bed to feed them. None of us really knew how bad things were for him in those last few months before he died. He was really struggling with depression and I believe he felt a great deal of shame for not being able to do the things he could.

In the end, it was a severe case of pneumonia that took his life, but it was his stubbornness and need to be strong and not rely on anyone that ultimately led to his sickness becoming life threatening and finally feeling like a failure and losing his will to live.

In 2019

Three years before my Dad passed away, I lost my Nan. She and I were really close and it felt like my world had shattered when she passed away. I think I cried every day for 6 months straight, and even now, I still find there are days that tears pour down my face. I miss her cheeky nature, her warm hugs, her famous jam drops which will never be baked the same again, the way she always tucked us into bed and always called on Sunday nights. She was an incredible woman and taught me everything I know about cooking and gardening and shared with me her love for wild birds and the Australian bush. She grew up in the years after the depression with little money for a large family — the children sleeping in drawers — and the expectation that as soon as you could, you would marry a man, get a job and fend for yourself. She lived a hard life for years on the road with my Pop driving trucks, running the books for the business, cooking and feeding everyone, raising a family, volunteering with Rural Ambulance and SES and contributing and supporting her local community any way she could. Her biggest weakness was her inability to say no and to prioritise herself.

For years I saw her as a hero, the epitome of strength. There was nothing she couldn't do and she would not stop at night until everyone else was fed, bathed and looked after. She got a great deal of joy from helping others and seeing her family and loved ones cared for and happy and even through her own challenges, she was the one who stood tall and strong holding everyone else up. As I grew older, I started to see that the strength she possessed was a false sense of strength and in fact her weakness. It was her inability to put boundaries in place and speak of her own desires and dreams. A common way of life for many women of her generation keeping the family dream and their husbands happy. My nan was a woman of few words spoken but possessed a great skill of poetry that shared many of her thoughts and stories of adventures and the way she saw the world. A beautiful collection that my family and I treasure.

In her final weeks before the cancer devoured what was left of her, I sat by her bedside, her hand in mine, weak and worn like an old tyre tread. I had spent those weeks with her, rubbing vitamin E cream into her legs, hands and arms, something I had watched her do my entire life and even in those moments when she was in so much pain, she would smile and give me a little squeeze. It broke my heart like I had never felt before to see this woman who was previously so capable, so physically strong, so knowledgeable and warm to be laying there like that. In her final weeks, while she could still speak all she was concerned about was making sure everyone else was OK. She barely complained and struggled to ask for help, succumbing to angry outbursts when she realised she couldn't do things herself and needed support. We were all there wanting to help her in any way we could as she had done for us our entire lives.

Nan was there for me for all of the special moments and knew exactly what to do in any circumstance. I remember her turning up to the photos before my wedding ceremony with bags of ice and buckets and me being really confused and if I'm honest a little embarrassed.

I had ordered tulips for my bouquets and had no idea that with a few hours out of the water, they would have resembled droopy broken stalks, but nan being nan and being the garden queen, she quickly jumped into action and gathered the ice and buckets and saved the day. It made the biggest difference and I will forever be grateful for everything she did that day and many others.

June 2009

Contained the hardest day of my life. I was just 22, and Nan was there by my side while I wrangled my two-and-a-half year old daughter out of the car and into the crematorium. We sat squished together, my hands shaking and my makeup already running down my face as she held me up while the ceremony took place, everyone still in disbelief that he was gone.

I remember the morning phone call at 2am: "Dan, he is gone," and I remember the last time we saw him and said our goodbyes the day before. At 27 years old, my daughter's father was gone, and my baby girl was without her dad.

He had been diagnosed with a rare and vicious cancerous tumour that was wrapping itself around his spinal column. After the decision to go ahead with surgery, he battled the horrid disease and excruciating pain with chemotherapy and radiation and strong painkillers. I witnessed him fade away, his body stripped of its life and in less than six months after his diagnosis and with all medical intervention exhausted he was told to go home, say his goodbyes and get his affairs in order. They gave him two weeks to two months and in the second week of being at home he passed away in his sleep.

Before his cancer diagnosis, he was full of life, a hard worker, a heavy metal drummer, the life of the party and a loving Dad. It broke all of our hearts when he left, and it took me six years to fully grieve and accept his loss. Having not lost anyone close to me before, it was a huge shock and the emotions, legalities, family and everything that came with it was overwhelming. The next few years were hell as I grieved my daughter's loss for a Dad she would not know. We speak of him often, share stories and his love for bad comedy and heavy metal and made sure she knew she was loved by him.

In 2013

On the fourth anniversary of his passing, my whole world came crashing down when my own grief finally caught up with me. For years, I had suppressed my own emotions, busy taking care of my daughter and getting through life. I had felt every sadness and emotion on my daughter's behalf and now it was time to mend my own heart. I was officially diagnosed with depression and anxiety panic disorder. I struggled to go to work and had random panic attacks and sleepless nights for months. It took me another two years, lots of counselling, psychology and antidepressants to get it under control. He was my first real love and each day I am reminded of the importance he played in my life, in my healing journey and the gift of my beautiful daughter with his same sense of humour.

The gifts

These have been some of the most defining moments of my life and taught me that

grief is the parting gift and proof that there is still love to give. It's a reminder that life is impermanent, that everything changes and ultimately that, we are here to experience it all. Sadly society has taught us that showing emotions is weak, however they are not weak nor strong. They are important messages to help us discern from what is aligned and what is not and along with the relationships we have, they serve us by offering the gift of reflection.

We are all on a learning and healing journey and one that is not a linear path, but instead a multifaceted collection of opportunities to bring us back to our truth so that we can live in our fullest expression of love for ourselves and others.

My journey, is an example of these opportunities and I hope it inspires and impacts you to shed your false strengths, speak your truth and open your heart to love, forgiveness and a life you were designed to live

I want to be remembered as a woman

- who embraced her weirdness and unique interests with curiosity and courage

- who faced her shadows and conditioning and rediscovered her truth
- who loved, respected and honoured her needs, desires and boundaries
- who let go of things and circumstances that were draining and out of alignment
- who listened to her body, rested and didn't apologise for her capacity
- who prioritised others as much as herself
- who asked for help and embraced her tribe without shame or the need to justify
- who trusted herself and practised being open without fear of criticism
- who embraced change and the gifts of trial and error
- who opened her heart to love, loss and new beginnings
- And who shared her story to support others on their journey

What do you want to be remembered for?

Ask yourself:

How can I honour myself and my truth even more?

How can I love and embrace my unique inner strengths?

How can I open myself and my heart to be the strongest version of me?

If you would like to learn about your unique energetic design or want some support in your deconditioning and unlearning journey, I would love to hear from you

Book a coaching call or Human Design Reading with me

Head to my website for details

www.wildflowwellbeing.com.au

About the Author

Hi, I'm Dani, the founder of Wild Flow Wellbeing & Wild Flow Kids.

I'm a wellbeing and empowerment coach, Human Design reader, nature lover, yogi and mum to a sixteen-year-old daughter from Brisbane, Australia.

I am passionate about supporting women, mums and their kids to slow down and reconnect with themselves and the world around them, and I believe that nature, mindfulness and really getting to know ourselves are the keys to a happier, healthier life.

I run nature yoga, mindfulness and craft programs for kids aged 2-12 years across Brisbane and offer human design readings and coaching to support those who need a little extra support and permission to be themselves again.

Website: www.wildflowwellbeing.com.au
Facebook: www.facebook.com/Wildflowwellbeing
Instagram: www.instagram.com/wildflowkids/

Debbie Smart

You don't choose a life – you live one

Every woman who heals herself helps heal all the women who came before her and all those who will come after – Dr Christine Northrup You don't choose a life – you live one!

My passion is My Health, My Mission (heal myself and others mind-body-spirit) and My Relationships, in that order because if I don't have my health, I can't fulfill my mission and I won't turn up bringing the best of myself to my relationships.

As I reflect on my story which is filled with both physical and emotional neglect, I can't help but think of the phrase "life is happening for you and not to you" and how the events of my past though difficult at the time have positively shaped the person I am today.

I was born in Johannesburg, South Africa the largest city and capital of Gauteng province. My mother Barbara Anna was from a conservative middleclass family, where her father, my grandfather Hermanus worked on the railways before he retired. Her mother, my grandmother Dorothy stayed home to take care of the family, but I got the impression that even though she had four children she wasn't much of the "mothering" type. She found it difficult to be confined to household duties and my mother would complain that she left most of the domestic chores to the girls.

Barbara was the second youngest of four siblings, three girls and one boy. She was quite different from the others and often referred to herself as the "Black Sheep" of the family. I recall her relationship with her mother was often fraught with a lack of understanding and criticism for the choices she made. My father Edgar on the other hand was from Germany and came to South Africa as a young man barely able to speak English. It was at the time many young people were leaving Europe in search of better opportunities. In some ways my parents would have shared some of the same ideologies and probably sought solace in each other at the time.

At the age of 25 my mother fell pregnant unexpectedly and while she was not young in the scheme of things, at the time it was frowned upon because she was not yet married. South Africa was an extremely conservative patriarchal society with not only challenges with racism, apartheid but also disparities against women. Women were not supported having children out of wedlock besides being a reflection on her family and something my grandmother never let her forget, so she decided marriage was appropriate.

The marriage was doomed from the start, and you could tell by my, father's behaviours how he resented the responsibility of a new family. It was obvious from the beginning he was struggling with the expectations of the traditional gender roles, societal expectations, and financial pressure which was overwhelming for a man who had little resilience based on his own emotional traumas from war-torn Europe. He struggled with the language and cultural differences too, and soon found himself in another relationship with a woman he knew growing up. He married her soon after and together they had another child – my half-brother Marcel.

My parents divorced when I was two and ironically my mother found herself on her own raising me after all, and with it came the challenges of single parenting. During the 60's Women in South Africa couldn't open their own bank accounts or let alone lease an apartment, there was no social security or facilities for very early childcare. She had to rely on my grandfather to help her out, he opened a banking account for her, put his name on the lease agreement but however made it very clear that she could not rely on them for much else. At one stage her eldest sister Myrtle offered to adopt me as she was in a secure marriage and had two daughters of her own, but my mother declined. I often wonder how different life would have been if that happened. Sadly, I don't have much to do with my extended family in South Africa, we drifted apart, and I suspect they distanced themselves because we didn't fit their mould.

Life was tough for Barbara because she would have to hold down two jobs to make ends meet, and at that time had to rely on public transport which wasn't the most reliable. She had employed an African Lady to take care of me during the day while she was at work, this lady would leave me in the apartment while she visited with friends. It was only when the neighbour told my mother this was happening, and I was crying all day that she was able to put a stop to it. I was around 9 months old at the time so reliant on her for my needs. What fascinates me is that I have an interesting relationship with food because of this, I notice how my body quickly shuts down when I feel stressed.

At the age of three I could finally go to a daycare or creche as they called it in South Africa. The creche had a bus service, so they would drop the children home each night aftercare. By this stage we had moved into the suburbs and my mother rented a cottage on a property which she found a bit easier as the rent wasn't as high, and I had a garden to play in. Barbara still didn't drive so relied heavily on public transport to get to and from work. One day her bus broke down coming home from work, usually she got home before me, to be there when the bus dropped me at home. There were no mobile phones in those days so not much she could do. The creche bus arrived and with no one at home put me over the wall and left me in the garden. My mother finally arrived home after dark to find me sitting against the wall exhausted, cold, and very frightened. I still have a vivid memory of that time and for a long time overreacted when I felt like I had been left behind. What I have come to realise is you never get over traumatic experiences you find ways to cope.

By the time I was 5 years old my grandparents thought it would be a good idea for us to come and live with them. They could help my mother out and she could help them as they were both getting older. I started school living with them, which made it easier on everyone as there was someone to look after me in the afternoons. (There was no after school-care in those days so yet another challenge my mother had to face). My mother found it difficult living with my grandparents as she felt my grandmother found fault in everything she did. By the time I was 8 we moved from my grandparents, and I was sent off to boarding school because that was the most practical option at that time.

I hated boarding school and was terribly homesick. I struggled to learn because I was so unhappy, and I remember how often I would get into trouble.

One of my most vivid memories is how we were pulled out of bed to kneel in the passage because the dormitory of 20 kids would not settle after the lights went out. On the last day of term, I got sick and recall how frightened I was because everyone was leaving school to go home for the holidays. Everyone had left and I was still at school sitting in front of a heater trying to get warm, thinking I may just be left here, and no one was coming to get me. I felt so unwell and alone that day before being collected, a common theme that was to show up a few times in my life.

We moved home a lot and by the time I was 10 I had gone to several different schools. I never settled down anywhere and always felt as though I didn't belong. I didn't try very hard at school either and didn't bother to put any effort into friendships because I knew it wouldn't be long before we would move on again. By this time Barbara had met and married another man Kurt, and we moved to Cape Town. Cape Town is a beautiful city on the southwest coast of South Africa and is well known for Table Mountain the flat-topped mountain that forms the significant landmark that overlooks the city. I was excited to go as I envisaged new beginnings, and the opportunity to be part of a family, something I so often dreamed about. Unfortunately, however it wasn't long before the cracks began to show up in that relationship and we found ourselves back in Johannesburg, my mother going through another divorce. Looking back the memories I have of my time in Cape Town were very lonely and I suffered from much anxiety because I was pulled yet again, into an adult's world with adult problems. My mother would use me as her confidante discussing the problems and frustrations she had with my stepfather. I was never sure what to do and didn't know how to fix it so was left feeling very unsettled and more of a burden to her which all played havoc with my self-worth.

On our return to Johannesburg, my mother and I went to live with her eldest sister and her husband, my aunt Myrtle and uncle Jim. They lived in a beautiful, thatched roof house out in the country. Both my cousins Felicity and Kathy had horses and I spent some weekends at the stables with them where they used to ride. They both went to a private girl's school and learnt to play the piano. I remember the grand piano in the living room wishing I could learn to play. My cousin Kathy also did ice skating, and Barbara was the one who would drive her to her skating lessons both in the morning and evenings.

Shortly after our return to Johannesburg my mother realised, she could not sustain this schedule and worry about me as well, so I went to a boarding school a second time, about 5 hours away. I would come home during the school holidays which was once every three months. I hated being away from home and would often cry to her on the phone, she did come up and visit me once a term and the school arranged a bus home three times a year which was a consolation. I remember the feeling I would get when I had to return to school and to this day, I feel the same way if I pack up to go somewhere. It hangs over me like a thick fog and takes the joy from me when I pack for holidays. I also get anxious if an alarm clock goes off because at boarding school we were woken up by a loud siren and bright lights, all the things I have worked through.

I clearly remember the day the accident happened; I was home for the school holidays and my cousin was driving a small ride on tractor towing a trailer. I was sitting on the edge of the trailer when she went over a mound, and I tumbled headfirst off the trailer and slipped in under it. She tried to stop but it was too late. They thought I had broken ribs but as not much could be done about it, I was just left to rest and heal on my own. I don't recall going to the hospital or ever having any x-rays.

Shortly thereafter I had to go into a back brace because it was discovered I had a scoliosis, honestly life couldn't have been much worse, the only consolation was that I had to leave boarding school and could be home. I began to see my father around this time too and spent school holidays with his family, his stepchildren from his wife's first marriage and my half brother Marcel. I felt so awkward visiting them, I hardly knew my father besides he worked most of the time, so days were spent with Lily my stepmother and her children. Going to my father was also a culture shock as I didn't speak German, and traditions like Christmas were quite different too. I really didn't know my father very well and by the time I was eighteen I decided I wasn't visiting any longer. The only reason he saw me was out of obligation and guilt so this time it was my call to drop him from my life. I just wanted to escape, my teenage years were very lonely and wearing a brace certainly did not help matters, I just disappeared further into my own world finding it hard to try and be accepted.

When I turned eighteen, I just wanted to work and have some independence to make my own choices. The shame I felt ran deep, I felt self-conscious about being flawed on many levels and no longer wanted to be a burden to my mother. I was a sensitive child and worked hard not to be an inconvenience, always hung back, and played small. I felt invisible and insignificant, besides I also wanted to move further away from my extended family who thought I would amount to nothing or turn out like my mother something my grandmother would often say to me.

In 1985, two years after finishing school I was accepted to do a nursing and midwifery diploma at the Johannesburg hospital. It was one of the best times in my life as I felt like I really belonged somewhere. I made many wonderful friends, and the nursing lecturers, gave me extra responsibilities and for the first time felt someone could see my worth. I was naturally a good nurse and loved the opportunity to work in such a large teaching hospital. I thrived in the environment where we were encouraged to not only use our initiative but to critically think and maintain best practice. During this time of my young adult life, I also met my husband Gordon and fell pregnant, and we married and went on to have three beautiful children, two girls and a boy.

We immigrated to Australia 23 years ago and lived in the Seychelles for two years before that giving our two eldest children a unique experience and some very special memories. I think back over our time in the Seychelles with mixed emotions and while it is a very beautiful Island, and most people would think an idyllic place to live, did have its problems. There is a large ex-patriot community living there and life was one big party, and not somewhere I wanted to live long term. I could see our opportunity to live in Australia slipping away so decided to leave my husband there and come to Australia on my own with our two young children.

It was not easy and found history repeating itself, a young single mother with two small children trying to rent somewhere to live. It was an opportunity to get a glimpse of challenges of my mother's life.

After completing his project Gordon joined us in Australia a year later and shortly after that our youngest child was born, we often would say she is very special because now our family has one child for me, one child for Gordon and we have one for the county. It was a flippant comment made by one of the political leaders at the time and seems we may have taken it literally but always grateful in how she cemented us to the Australian culture and the place we now call home. Truly she is a gift, all my children are as they have been my greatest teachers.

My adult life has not been without its challenges but it's the part of my life I had more control of, and upon reflection I feel a deep sense of satisfaction in most of the decisions I have made but also importantly the ones Gordon and I have made together. We have been married for 34 years and while it was not without its difficulties and a separation we have worked together for the greater good of our family and found healing in the longevity of our relationship. Our three beautiful adult children have a secure sense of who they are, emotional stability and very successful in their own right, of which I am very proud and is no doubt my greatest achievement. We now expect our first grandchild in December 2023 and overjoyed that our legacy will live on in stable secure relationships.

Life never quite turns out in ways you would expect, and sadly while I have lost both my parents, my half-brother Marcel and I find comfort in getting to know each other better. We both stand intentionally breaking the wounds of our past knowing that it's in relationship and going to those painful places that transformation takes place.

I have always known I must have been born for a greater purpose much like us all so this does not come from an arrogant place but rather a deep yearning to know if I healed, the world would heal with me. The saying used often "we are a spiritual being having a human experience" made such sense and my understanding that we choose our experience to grow and evolve is my truth. I know the importance of paying attention to mind-body-spirit based on this spiritual understanding so chose a university that took into consideration the mind and spirit of healing. The physical body I knew because of my background in nursing. Through my counselling degree I learned to explore my emotional neglect and gaps in my learning and development. When it came to study and focus, I presented with symptoms of ADHD, however due to my knowledge and further investigations, it turned out that anxiety and a dysregulated central nervous system was the cause. This could well be the case for many others, so frequently diagnosed with this condition and then given medication. The treatments I used took longer and required patience but with consistent action the results have been amazing. I help my clients with various modalities for results, together with the Human Design and Ayurveda road map, which brings a deeper level of understanding of who you are, what you are designed for and how you can heal mind-body-spirit.

To end off my story I would like to acknowledge my family and in particular my husband Gordon who has unflinchingly supported me in my journey.

About the Author

Debbie Smart is an experienced Psychotherapist and Emotional/Spiritual Coach who has a special interest in Central Nervous System regulation, understanding energy and emotional vibration. She is an expert in Human Design and the Gene Keys and has helped many find their purpose and a deeper level of self awareness.

While Debbie brings her formal qualifications in Health and Counselling/Psychotherapy she also brings a wealth of life experience and knowledge of energy work to her practice. She is passionate about deepening her own spiritual journey through yoga, meditation and spending time in nature. Debbie loves to travel and stretch herself taking on new experiences, walking the Camino Santiago being one of them.

Email: debbieannecouselling@gmail.com
Instagram/Facebook: debs.smart and Debbie Smart
Website: www.debbiesmart.com

Megan Smith

May we all learn to fully trust our intuition, so that we can hear the whispers and be guided by them

I had felt this feeling before. When your stomach drops with dread, your heart starts to break, tears pool in your eyes, and you feel nauseous. I bet that you have felt something similar at some point in your life. This was the same feeling when I was 20-yrs-old, and I received a phone call with the heart-shattering news that my dad had committed suicide. At age 30, I felt the feeling again. The words my mum spoke through the phone are those you never want to hear, "I have cancer".

Intuition is your soul whispering the truth to your heart and hoping that you hear. The horrible feeling was masked as my intuition sent me a message. It wasn't a whisper like it is for everyday decisions which we can fail to see the significance of. It was a roar to my heart. It was telling me to travel home to be with my Mum. One day I was working on board a mega yacht in Florida with my then-boyfriend, having the time of my life.

Days later, I was by my mum's side in Australia as she recovered from losing a third of her left lung.

Soon after Mum's surgery, I returned to yachting. It didn't feel right anymore, and the nomadic magic started to fade. As an only child who had been travelling the world for 10 years, I craved being able to hug her and spend quality time together. Facetime allowed Mum and I to see each other almost every day on a screen but it wasn't enough. I couldn't ignore the feeling that I was ready to leave my adventurous yachting lifestyle behind me to settle down and make a home in Australia. Even though my boyfriend at the time was reluctant to leave our life on the sea behind, my intuition had spoken, and I listened. We made the move together and began our new chapter of life on land.

Life on the Gold Coast was everything I had hoped for in the beginning. Simple, fun, routine, and close enough that I could visit Mum regularly. My boyfriend, however, had a hard time finding his way. We accepted that it was part of the transition home. A couple of years passed, the simple became mundane and our goal to buy a home didn't materialise. It felt as though we were very much separate. We had good times, but rarely did we didn't do anything or go anywhere together. I felt like I was constantly trying to be supportive, and positive and it was hard work. I thought this was how love was. My intuition spoke in whispers telling me to leave many times, however, I chose not to trust this, listening to my conscious reasoning instead. We had been together for years; I didn't want to give up on us or feel alone. Instead of following my intuition and trusting everything would be okay, I looked for connections elsewhere and found an inspiring group of friends when I embarked on my networking marketing journey. My focus turned to learning a new skill, reconnecting with my outgoing personality, and stepping out of my comfort zone with the support of a positive group of change-makers. It was also a time when I was introduced to the world of personal development.

Between visiting Mum and my new positive community, the divide grew greater between my then boyfriend and I, and we carried on as 'normal'.

"Cancer is like a seed which is thrown into a garden. You never know where it will sprout next". Mum, my stepdad, and I were given this analogy by the oncologist during one of Mum's check-ups. Her cancer had returned and was terminal. "Some people live for 2 years, some 20," we were told by the same oncologist. All I remember is that awful feeling returning, and I sobbed as my mum sat there and nodded. It looked like acceptance, but I now know she took it as a challenge to live for 20 years. From that moment on, Mum stopped drinking and smoking with the flick of a switch. She said she just knew that for her to have the best chance of survival, this was what she needed to do. She was listening to her intuition.

Our visits with each other became more regular and so did Mum's chemotherapy treatments. Doctors were continuously astounded by her positive mental attitude. They attributed this to the reason why she continued to live a relatively normal life over the next few years. As time progressed, there was no denying her health was declining slowly. We never made it a topic of conversation for long, we simply adjusted our activities during our time together. It was a constant lingering feeling at the pit of my stomach knowing that I would eventually lose my mum, my cheerleader. I could never do wrong in my Mum's eyes, and she always told people how wonderful I am and how proud she is of me.

I feel fortunate to have always been shown and felt love in my life, although I haven't always loved myself. I was introduced to MJB Seminars, a Perth-based personal growth coaching and transformational course company through my network marketing company at the time.

Their guidance has been invaluable in my journey to understanding myself and events throughout my life. I harboured abandonment issues when my dad took his life and I felt as though I wasn't enough for him to live for. I was angry at him and thought him a coward for a long time. MJB Seminars helped me to understand that life happens for me, not to me. Where there is darkness, there is always light and nothing is ever lost, it changes form. Investing in personal development can benefit all areas of your life, especially when you feel a positive energy with whom you decide to work. It can lead to life-changing shifts, -like what I experienced.

I was able to reflect on past events and see them from a different perspective. My dad instilled a wanderlust in me and without his passing, I would not have had the funds initially to embark on my backpacking journey which led me to work and travel around the world. Dad was not a coward for taking his life. I understand how hard it must have been for him to make the last phone call to his only child when he knew it was the last time we would ever speak. What a courageous man. My stepfather became the person in my life who provided the same emotional connection I had with my dad. The ability to feel gratitude for an event occurring in life, no matter how devastating, is the most liberating feeling.

The bad news, nothing lasts forever. The good news, nothing lasts forever. Five years had passed since Mum's terminal news was delivered to us in the specialist's office. My stepdad phoned advising that Mum was admitted to hospital with pneumonia. She was a typical mum, not wanting anyone to make a fuss but secretly loved when you did. I surprised her with a visit. She had become more tired, given up work and her appetite had decreased. Her spirits were high, but her body was frail. My intuition whispered and I listened. I needed to find a way to be with her full-time. I am so grateful I was in the position to be able to take extended leave from my career and they held my role open for 6 months. I had no reason to believe that I wouldn't return.

Don't let the hard days win. My days were all about being a support for Mum in her home. Taking her to doctor appointments, chemotherapy, understanding the medications, cooking and just being together. Her walking turned into being wheelchair-bound. There were nights when she would cough continuously. I felt selfish thinking it would be better for her to be taken from us. I would lay by her side and rub her back and just be with her for comfort. Mother and daughter.

The trouble is you think you have time. Two months into my six months stay, Mum had trouble breathing and was admitted to hospital. The dreaded feeling that constantly lurked in my stomach became prominent. I stayed with her during the day and slept in her room at night. Mum called me brave for staying, but I could not bear to leave her. The medication to ease her pain slowly consumed her. She became unconscious and communication was lost. All I wished was for her to make a miraculous recovery. Part of me still didn't believe this was reality. I sat with her watching TV one night, chatting to her knowing she could hear me. I remembered, where there is darkness, there is light. Life is happening for me. Nothing is ever lost, it changes form. I knew what I had to do. With love, I said to her, "If you want to go it's okay, I understand. I'm proud of you, proud to be your daughter, and wouldn't change it for the world. You have fought hard". I felt at peace. I knew that everything was going to be okay. Within two minutes, she exhaled her last breath, and she was at rest.

Even if you know what's coming, you're never prepared for how it feels. Being with Mum as she passed was an experience of simultaneous emotions. Loving and heart-shattering, honour, disbelief, but grateful that I could be by her side. Afterwards, I was often questioned how I was dealing with the passing of my mum so well and it made me feel as though something was wrong with me. I felt sadness and cried, but the pain was over for her and that was a relief.

The most important relationship in your life is with yourself. The obvious next step was to go back to my partner, job, and life on the Gold Coast. I didn't want to return to that reality straight away. The thought of leaving made me feel deflated and anxious. I decided to stay and help my stepdad in his painting business. We were each other's support as we adjusted to our new reality without Mum.

Life happens when you make plans. My mum and stepdad had purchased their home, a catamaran many years before to explore Queensland's beautiful islands. It never came to fruition because life got busy, then Mum was diagnosed with cancer and her chemotherapy was too regular to allow them such an adventure.

I came up with the idea that in a year's time, my stepdad and I should take the boat exploring.

Upon my return to the Gold Coast, driving on a Sunday afternoon down the main street, I casually put the idea to my boyfriend and for him to come along. He rejected the idea and was taken aback when I told him that I would be going.

The boat trip was amazing. We took Mum's ashes with us and spoke to her every day as if she was with us. It was bittersweet and the memories we made are so dear to my heart.

If you want something different, do something different. Meditation is not a regular practice of mine, but I felt called to it on this day. I sat on the beach under a palm tree, closed my eyes, and pressed play on the insight timer, meditation. The calming male voice went silent as the meditation ended and I had clarity. My thoughts weren't clouded by conscious reasoning of emotions or fear. My intuition whispered and I listened.

That day my long-term relationship ended, and I embarked on a new life.

Mum's passing gifted me the opportunity and permission to experience my circumstances through a different lens. I had chosen not to trust my instincts when it came to my relationship for a long time. This was a reminder that your intuition whispers your truth, be cautious if you choose not to harness it.

I have also found that when intuition whispers feel too faint to hear, I have some alone time in a calming place and ask myself two questions. What would I do if my decision only affected me and what would I do if time and money were no object? These questions allow me to move from my head space into my heart space.

Opportunities are out there everywhere, and you never know where they will lead you. To take advantage, requires you to be brave and step outside of your comfort zone. A perceived challenge of the network marketing industry, is reaching out and connecting with people with the hope that they will see value in what you have to offer and that it will benefit them like it has you. Scrolling on Facebook a few years back when I had just started my journey, I came across an old friend that I used to party with almost 20 years prior. He was in good shape which was a good indicator that he might like the products I shared, so I added him as a friend. Turns out he wasn't interested in what I had and that was that.

Fast forward to my new life, in my new town, and enjoying my newfound love of painting. All which came to me from listening to my intuition and trusting that life is happening for me, I receive a message from him asking if I would like to have a catch-up for old times' sake as we were now in the same town. This man is now my husband. Life is always working for us. In the twists and turns along our journey, what we need is presented to us as the future unfolds. It may not make sense, but in time, all is revealed. I would not have found the network marketing industry if it were not for my mum becoming sick. Being surrounded by a positive community has been pivotal in encouraging me to show up as a positive light each day for those who may need it.

Death can be perceived as a tragedy in life. If my mum had not passed away, I would not be married and experienced the kind of love that lights me up. I would not be able to work alongside my stepdad in our painting business and enjoy the family time which is so precious. I would not have been able to support friends in seeing the light in the darkness when their loved ones passed away.

To get through the hardest journey, take one step at a time, but keep on stepping. My journey of listening to my intuition isn't always perfect. Clarity is easily lost as emotions, memories, and reasons interrupt messages from the heart. Our inner truth remains unheard and waits for the next opportunity to present itself. Each time I share my story with others, I can see their mind retracing their timeline finding moments when they can relate. I realised that everyone has their own unique story which they may not share. Positive, aligned action is halted by perceived fears and limitations.

I have so much adoration for the network marketing industry, and to so many, the magic remains unshared and misunderstood. It has given me the most connection, friendship, empowerment, and positivity throughout my life. It is exciting creating my success from the ground up and supporting others to do the same in an open and nurturing way. One of my favourite things about life is meeting new people and listening to their journeys. By sharing my own story, my wish is to continue connecting with driven women. Those who embody heart-based possibility with the belief they are capable and deserving of being emotionally and financially self-sufficient. Watch them step into their power and stand on their own two feet by tuning in to their intuition to walk the path of their choosing.

The sun will rise and set regardless. What we choose to do with the light while it shines is up to us. I have opened myself up to the opportunity to speak with audiences worldwide. Not as a professional, but as a woman inspiring other women, that ordinary is extraordinary. Comparison is the thief of happiness. You don't need to be an influencer or public figure to have a voice of impact. I am a regular woman, living a regular life, finding my way to do the best I can. We all have a voice of impact within us, it is our intuition.

About the Author

Megan Smith grew up in a small town in Central Queensland, Australia. Family holidays abroad seeded her passion to continue exploring the world.

Spending over a decade abroad, Megan's experience with travel, life, love, and death eventually brought her back to Australia, finding her paradise in Yeppoon, Queensland. She lives with her family and puppy, Frankie.

A lover of the ocean, outdoors, and making memories with friends and family, Megan also finds fulfilment in connecting with women around the world through her positive online presence.

Email: megsmith@outlook.com.au
Facebook: www.facebook.com/megan.shorrocks.7
Website: msha.ke/megsmith

Cat Spratt

As you read this chapter, I invite you to feel into and reflect upon your own life's journey. How has your inner wisdom guided you?

Looking back, the signs to my soul's true expression have been there throughout my life. Subtle glimpses to the world I was yet to explore and integrate, and huge whopping bops over the head, that I of course ignored at the time!

As everyone in this world, I wear many hats. A mother, woman, wife, sister, daughter, friend, energy worker, soul intuitive…the list goes on. But beneath all the many hats is a soul. A soul that is yearning to be expressed.

As I navigate this life with all my hats on, participating actively and as an observer, I see an interweaving of different aspects. This life 'thing', it truly is bigger than me and you as we see it.

Everything is connected, our emotions, feelings, mind, body, past versions of ourselves, our best selves, future selves, true selves, and of course our relations with others, our environment, natural cycles, the universe...energy.

Everything is connected.

My mother passed away after a short illness when I was 22. Most of us are not guided on how to release from emotional experiences, and a part of me shut down that day.

At the time of her passing it was like I was viewing the world through a glass window, and that this wasn't my life. I couldn't understand grief. I, for sure, dissociated with my feelings and found myself going straight into the "doing-not-dealing" mode. For me, the "doing-not dealing" mode was a distraction, a coping mechanism. Stopping me from sitting with my feelings and allowing them to pass through, be understood, realised, and even released.

I repeated this subtle pattern of "doing-not-dealing" through the years to follow.

A familiar mode of life that I now see presenting in many of my clients.

Around 10 years ago, I was drawn to study holistic massage. I was so used to following structure or a pre trodden path hailed to succeed like previous academic experiences, which when didn't go to plan or felt difficult, left me depleted, deflated, and to be honest, cynical. Therefore, initially it felt quite alien to allow myself that intuitive freedom that the course guided, and to trust, well, me! Trust soon flowed and a door opened to tapping into my own intuitive gifts. I will always be so grateful to my incredible tutors for introducing me to the beautiful art, intuitive freedom, and healing powers of massage.

Shortly after this time, I was in a different job with massage as an uncommitted side hustle. I was feeling anxious and overwhelmed, over-exercising, on the go all the time and generally looking to be something and someone outside of myself. Buying into societal pressures and life path expectations. I was experiencing recurrent UTIs where courses of antibiotics weren't touching, and at one point gave me an allergic reaction where my body could barely move. The pain and discomfort experienced were always at the forefront of my mind. One flippant remark from a medical practitioner saying "there isn't much you can do about it" without any further guidance or support was unhelpful and disparaging. Nothing I could do about it...

Or so I thought.

To add into the mix, around this time I experienced three devastating miscarriages. Grieving, depleted, unable to give the desired energy and focus to work, family, or friends, I felt alone and fearful in this experience and underwhelmed with life.

I was so far connected to who I was and wanted to be.

My body a separate entity, crying out for help, and I didn't know how to listen.

It was a grief resurfacing from 13 years prior. I didn't fully understand the feelings, let alone process them.

Have you ever found a time in your life where you didn't fully understand your feelings and how to process them?

I know I didn't until one day I happened upon an advert for a local wellness course and signed up. On arrival, I realised with wonder and tingles of excitement, that this was far beyond your average 5-a-day wellness, there was a depth to concepts that resonated to the core and shouted "YES! This is what I need in my life!".

Have you ever experienced those tingles, those gut feelings that with every fibre of your being feels so right for you?

This for me was my intuition guiding me towards Ayurveda, The "Science of Life". I knew that the doors had been opened further to a new way of life. Ayurveda, a lifestyle roadmap that creates harmony across body, mind, and soul. It has this gentle essence of nourishment, one that allows us to experience wholesome wellness.

I spoke to the Practitioner leading the course and was guided with a bespoke Ayurvedic treatment and lifestyle plan. My journey with holistic health had started. My UTI symptoms soon disappeared (hurrah!). I was taking back control; I was becoming empowered in my healing.

"How were the Ayurvedic principles not "mainstream" and adopted alongside Western medicine?" I thought. This would be the ultimate health combination! I just had to learn to become a practitioner for myself so I could share and support more people!

And that is just what I did.

During the course I became pregnant with my daughter. The timing seemed metaphorically a poetic re-birth, of myself, and the circle of life from the loss of my mother through to the birth of my daughter.

It was like each step of the way I was being gently guided to help me connect, heal, and release. And beyond this, I was starting to remember who I was at my very core. I was embracing the intuitive gifts I had been keeping stuffed down (I always have the vision of likening this to trying to stuff a sleeping bag into its tiny bag!!) and connecting with my body again.

Gratitude was at my core. I was grateful for so much at this time, including my unborn baby, this way of life, my improved health... I started writing down each day things I was grateful for. I thought I would run out of gratitudes, but they kept flowing and with those, synchronicities popped into my world each day.

Below, is a gentle gratitude practice I would like to share with you to take the feeling of gratitude into your day.

***

Gratitude practice

Find a comfortable place for your body, whatever that looks like for you.

Placing one hand on your heart space, start to feel the warmth and connection between the hand and chest.

Allow the gentle rise and fall of the chest to become the focus of the mind as you breathe gently in and out through the nose.

You may wish to lower the gaze or close your eyes as you continue following the gentle rhythm of the breath.

Allow any tension around the jaw to release, the shoulders relaxing fully.

Feel into this moment, present with the breath.

You may wish to think of something that you are grateful for in your life. It can be anything at all or even someone.

Then, perhaps consider why you are grateful.

What does this gratitude feel like for you in your body? What emotions does it bring up for you? If it feels good, can you cultivate that feeling or emotion and sit with it for a while?

Allow it to radiate through your whole body.

Continue for as long as you wish.

When you are ready, allow one last deeper inhale and exhale.

Gently lift the gaze or opening your eyes, take the feeling of gratitude into your day.

***

At this time, I was starting to embody Ayurveda and guide others, however I still felt there was something missing, a yearning for something that my mind's understanding was yet to fully integrate and put into practice...

It was during 2020, the year of the Pandemic, and I was raising my beautiful rainbow baby, adapting the Ayurvedic lifestyle to family life. I spent time connecting to and embracing my intuition through meditation, spending time in nature and integrating yoga. I was tapping into my soul's gifts and purpose in this world as a mother, a woman, and an energetic being.

I began to truly heal. Finding the missing pieces of the puzzle… **energy, frequency, and vibration**… I started to understand the real power behind my thoughts and beliefs, including the realisation that I also had the power to create my own experience.

What a revelation!

What then blossomed was quite astounding and incredibly rapid. The floodgates, never mind the doors, were now wide open.

A fire burned inside of me to guide and share with others.

My heart centred business, Soul Blossom, was birthed.

The essence of Soul Blossom, and specifically my bespoke programme, *Roots to Blossom*, is to truly nourish women. To honour them where they are, acknowledge their journeys, individual life experiences and womanhood. To see them as beautifully unique, as well as one that is connected. For them to feel safe in the knowledge they aren't alone or lost in this world. To help them come home to who they are.

I am specifically here to support those who feel overwhelmed or anxious around daily life. For those who feel they are here to experience something more, even if they aren't sure what this is yet. For those who feel subpar in their body and mind and are searching for a bespoke approach to their health and wellness, and a deeper connection with themselves again.

Every week I see beautifully unique, everyday women, just like me, experience healing and life at a deeper, more profound, and meaningful level, tapping into intuition and embodying their true selves.

It's been there all along; simply requiring the space and nourishment to grow.

Together, we remove blocks and guide the changes internally within their mind and body, externally in their environment, and subsequently the world!

Women stepping into their power.

Here are a couple of examples of clients I've worked with.

Client A came to me at a particularly stressful time in her life. She was overwhelmed, anxious and difficulty sleeping. She was in a demanding corporate role and felt obligated to work most days and evenings. A difficult situation with a colleague was encroaching into her thoughts. She divulged that she was at breaking point and looking for ways to manage anxiety. After an initial discussion to review options of working together, she embarked on the *Roots to Blossom* programme. My client travelled a lot, so it was important that the programme allowed for flexibility in location and length to suit her requirements.

We started with an Ayurvedic consultation which helped outline her goals and highlight what was fully going on in her experience across body, mind, and life in general. Her treatment plan was bespoken to her experience and included a holistic focus across dietary, daily activities, routine and herbal nourishment.

Regular distance reiki sessions helped her sleep and shift any rising anxiety, alongside access to weekly online yoga sessions and personal meditations, re-connecting her to the present moment and her body.

The subsequent weeks were interesting, as we started accessing her Akashic records for her Soul Readings, she started to notice positive shifts and opportunities arise. These helped her to start rediscovering her soul gifts, remove subconscious blocks and understand how to create her experience.

This all resonated to her current and life experience so much so that I was guided to teach her how to connect closely with her intuition using tools for her own healing and to help her create her desired reality. My client started to realise how naturally intuitive she is and how easily things had previously manifested for her, but that she hadn't been tapping into this ability with intention.

Now she has the tools and knowledge alongside her acknowledged intuition to embrace and create with intention!

Manifestations have happened that have dramatically improved her life experience.

Her sleep has improved, her anxiety reduced, and she now feels she is in control with her daily routine, work schedule and relationship boundaries. She can function with increased energy, make decisions with clarity, and her work day-to-day flows with ease.

Client B contacted me remotely after years of dieting with inconsistent and unsustainable results. She was a naturally intuitive woman running her own business and mother to 4 children living in the US.

Her previous Soul Reading with me resonated on several levels guiding her to embrace her soul gifts rather than diminishing them, allowing her to embrace these in her work and family life and clear energetic blocks in her experience. She mentioned that although she felt a lot of the previous experiences of anxiety had subsided since the reading, she had thought she was entering the perimenopausal stage. She had started to notice changes in her internal cycles, gain "stubborn" weight and felt frustrated with how she looked, how tired she had felt and unmotivated to engage in daily activities. The years of trying different diets had left her feeling overwhelmed and uncertain on what was the right course of action for her. Her aim was to have more energy, to enjoy spending outdoor time with her family and to not have to cook separate things for herself than that of her family.

The Ayurvedic consultation package was the most attractive for her situation, and following a consultation, I created a bespoke treatment plan tailored for her, detailing a gentle 3-day detox, herbal support, and dietary advice with a full explanation as to its suitability for her.

We then supplemented with yoga classes tailored specifically for her to help balance the hormonal changes, increase energy, and encourage gentle weight management. We made this fun and the short, recorded practices were able to fit around her busy day.

Due to the nature of the dietary and exercise focus, this helped her become more in tune with her cycles and relieved symptoms. As such she felt energised, empowered in her meal choices (which were also family friendly), her exercise routine improved, and she is now maintaining a healthy weight.

She is intuitively choosing activities and foods that flow with her lifestyle and internal cycle. This has given her more confidence, clarity, and ease in the choices that she makes daily regarding her health and family. Her family are also embracing the positive changes she has made.

***

The simplest actions are often the most effective!

I have created a short booklet outlining '*5 ways to connect with your intuition*'. In the booklet there are some simple ways you can start exploring connecting to your true self. I have also allowed for journal space and affirmations to help guide you on your way!

To receive your copy head over to my website (www.soulblossom.uk) and receive yours now!

***

What have I discovered so far that I would love to share with you?

I have found that **boundaries are essential.** Time and people boundaries are great places to start in exploring boundaries. Tuning into what feels healthy and sustainable for you. I find when I put boundaries in place, I am showing up for me and saying, "I am worthy of this experience". This makes me happy and feels safe and healthy for those around me too. Discipline comes into it a little to start with but then it starts to flow more easily.

Take a look at your current boundaries. How do they feel?

I am **embracing the uniqueness of myself and others.** Re-discovering my gifts, especially as an empath and semi-introvert, and to share these was incredibly profound (and a little daunting!). Confidence is growing daily. I am honouring my own path and finding a way that feels aligned for me.

I don't have to fit into a premade box!

You can normally find me with my hair scrapped back in a mum bun (heard this phrase recently and I have totally stolen it!), and wearing comfy leggings whilst performing energetic healings, massage treatments and leading programmes!

As I further step into this acceptance, I am becoming more understanding of the experience of others. Allowing space for myself and others to express and be.

Have a think about how beautifully unique you are. How can you embrace it?

I am **more connected to myself, nature's cycles and the natural flow of life**. I know when to bloom, to be out there connecting with others, and when to retreat and rest up. As a mother the knowing doesn't always coincide with my needs at the time (*can anyone else relate*?!), but I allow myself to trust, to make aligned choices and come into the present moment. My care of self within my life allows me to grow a resilience for when finding time for self is more challenging. I have my favourite go-to's such as self-massage, yoga, energy healing, gratitude practice and meditation.

But these are flexible.

There is an ebb and flow to allow for what I need and when.

What does self-care look like for you? Or what do you think would feel good for you right now?

As I continue forwards with the work that I'm doing, my mission is to **empower** more women, to **guide** and **witness** them thrive and experience **healthy, happy and extraordinary lives.**

If you are ready to blossom and thrive in your life, you can join my 1-1 *Roots to Blossom* programme or register for my upcoming group programme *Illuminate*!

I really have to say, it lights me up to be raising my daughter at this time. I am excited to continue **embracing the present moment** and having **gratitude** for where I am and what the day holds. Each day truly is a **gift** and offers opportunities for **growth.**

I know I will be **gently guided** on my next steps along my life path. I **trust** the timing.

And my wish is for you to trust it too.

About the Author

Cat is the owner of Soul Blossom, a holistic and heart centred business. She is an Energy Healer, Holistic therapist and Soul Intuitive. Raised in Manchester, she now resides on the South Coast of the UK with her husband and daughter.

Cat has empowered, inspired, and changed the lives of hundreds of women. Guiding them to restore harmony across body, mind, and soul, giving them the clarity and confidence to re-discover and celebrate their beautiful and unique selves in their lives.

Cat's knowledge, together with her gentle intuition and holistic approach, allows women to feel at ease, supported on their wellbeing journey and soul re-discovery.

Cat loves connecting with nature, spending time at the beach, and kayaking with the family.

Linktr.ee: linktr.ee/soulblossom.uk
Facebook, Instagram: @soulblossomuk
Website: www.soulblossom.uk

Rene Thompson

When I was a little girl, my dad used to recite a poem that started with "One fine day, in the middle of the night, two dead men got up to fight..." It struck my quirky sense of humour as a child and sticks with me, now into my 54th year. It was a strange foreshadowing of my life: Feeling like I was living in the dark, even on bright, sunny days.

Anxiety was a familiar companion. It was only in my very early years that I don't remember its presence. But from around five years of age, I remember being on edge, my heart racing, afraid of everyone and everything. My go-to stress response was not 'fight' or 'flight' but a form of 'freeze' that saw me put my head down, do what was required and wishing to be invisible. However, we were a musical family, conspicuous because of our Australian/American accents, with a foot in two continents and a platform from which to perform.

From these very early days, I felt the pressure to help others to feel accepted and comfortable while I wanted to hide away: A sensitive, introverted child in an extrovert world.

From puberty, the darkness had descended like a cloud, casting a shadow over every day. While others experienced a wide range of emotions, from extreme highs to deep lows, my emotional scale seemed stuck like I was living in a constant state of "Meh" or worse.

All that emotional pain eventually took a toll on my body: Stomach-aches, muscle aches, shooting pains down my back and legs, terrible menstrual cramps and near-constant bleeding, and a never-ending headache. I didn't have the words to describe what was happening inside me and since I was in the habit of 'not rocking the boat', I didn't demand to be heard. So, I tried to push my own needs aside and focused on helping others instead, hoping that by turning my attention away from myself, I might find some relief.

Little did I know, I had unknowingly become a magnet for those who needed help. Broken souls, hurt people, and self-absorbed folks seemed to flock to me, hoping to dump their burdens onto someone else. My husband observed on more than one occasion, "You sure attract messed up people, don't you?" I didn't know how to set boundaries, so I often felt taken advantage of, even though I genuinely wanted to comfort those in distress. I was simply trying to be for others what I needed for myself.

Even with a loving husband and two amazing kids, I constantly felt overwhelmed, like I was drowning in it all. From the outside, our life seemed exciting—frequently moving houses, exploring new places, and starting fresh. Because I was so out of touch with my own needs, I didn't know how much I longed for stability and a sense of belonging. I needed roots to grow and a real home to call my own. I needed rest.

So, there I was, putting on a brave face, attending social events, and even singing on stage. But deep inside, I was as confused as anyone else. The messages I got from the doctors I saw over the years were always "There's nothing wrong with you", "It's all in your head", "Just take a break." I started believing what was suggested; that maybe I was just choosing to be negative. So, I pushed my struggles aside even more and pretended to be positive. "Fake it til you make it", right? I never made it.

While I never considered ending my life (I think now it was because I was too exhausted), the thought of not waking up became a recurring dream. I would jolt awake with a surge of adrenaline at the sound of a baby crying or an alarm, only to burst into tears because I had to face another day. I hid my tears and frustration, embarrassed that I couldn't handle life's challenges like everyone else. What was wrong with me?

In my early forties, I reached a breaking point. I couldn't stand the fake facade I had become. I felt pulled in every direction, feeling that everyone and everything demanded something from me. My heart raced, and my sleep suffered from palpitations. I sought medical advice, not specifically for my mood or anxiety, but because now I had a genuine physical concern which was, in my mind, more of a legitimate issue to bring before a doctor.

Within just five minutes, the doctor handed me a prescription for antidepressants and told me I would need them for life. He diagnosed me with Smiling Depression, a term I had never heard before. It meant that I had mastered the art of hiding my pain behind a smile. It turned out I wasn't crazy—I was just running on empty. Very, very empty.

I felt completely numb, standing at the pharmacy counter with my prescription in hand. The pharmacist handed me the box of pills, but on the way home, a thought crossed my mind—maybe there was another way. As a former nurse, I knew there were basic things I should do to support my good health that I was not doing. So, I made a decision: I would give myself six months to start implementing healthy habits before resorting to medication. If I still needed them, I would absolutely take those pills.

From as far back as I could remember, I had a constant craving for carbohydrates, and I relied on sugars and caffeine to keep me going. But now, I made a conscious effort to cut down on both and incorporate more fresh vegetables into my diet. I also knew I needed to exercise, so I impulsively bought a gym membership, thinking that "no pain, no gain" was the way to go.

Given my persistent exhaustion, high-intensity exercise only depleted my non-existent energy stores and left me drained for days. Often, a gentle walk around the local botanic gardens was all I could manage. Little did I know that this type of energy-giving exercise was precisely what I needed.

But I didn't give up. While there were no overnight miracles, I began to notice a subtle shift. Surprisingly, I never ended up taking those pills. My mood gradually improved as my body grew stronger, although it was a frustrating and painful journey, taking one step forward and one step back. But I kept going. It was the only hope I had, and I wasn't about to give up on it.

Looking back on those early years of my healing journey, I discovered that by focusing on my physical health, I inadvertently brought my mind and emotions back into balance. This valuable lesson now informs my work with clients. As I nourished and cared for my body with whole, real food and regular movement, and other essential health-supporting practices, my mind and heart also began to heal. It was an unexpected and wonderful side effect that I hadn't anticipated. All I had initially focused on was eating well and exercising every day. It wasn't until about five years later that I intentionally worked on finding balance in my mind and heart, now that my physical strength could support that journey. In the past, I simply didn't have the strength to address the dark cloud hanging over my head.

Making changes to the basic habits such as what we eat and how we move is undeniably challenging. I didn't know anyone else who saw health the way I did. My husband and children were not yet on board, and some well-meaning family members thought it would be helpful to ridicule the changes I was making or parroted mainstream health advice that only served as a constant reminder of how isolated I felt on my healing journey.

As I gained knowledge about nutrition and experienced the transformation in my own body, I eagerly shared what I had learned with anyone willing to listen.

I yearned to offer hope to others who were in the darkness, just as I had been, but I had yet to learn that many people simply are not willing to hear that they can take responsibility for their own health. It didn't take long to figure out who were the people with ears for my message and who were not.

However, as time passed and I developed connections that supported my newfound healthy habits, my habits became a lifestyle and my healing rate increased. My husband eventually jumped on the bandwagon too after witnessing the toll chronic illness took on our extended family. Together, we made a pact that our lives would be different. We vowed never to return to the eating and lifestyle habits that lead to such illnesses, regardless of how many so-called "experts" encouraged it.

I made a firm decision never to take health advice from someone who clearly wasn't well themselves. Would you trust financial advice from someone who repeatedly filed for bankruptcy? Or seek marriage advice from someone with multiple divorces? Common sense tells us to consider the source, doesn't it?

The problem in our society today is that we often fail to recognize the signs of ill-health until we receive a diagnosis. And even then, we too often resign ourselves to the belief that it's incurable. But I call hogwash on that notion. There's always another doctor, another perspective. I refuse to accept a life sentence that way. A diagnosis is merely a label for a collection of symptoms—it tells you how high the mountain is that you have to climb.

Eventually, I found health professionals who embraced a holistic approach, looking beyond the symptoms for the root cause and supporting the body's innate ability to heal. Integrative and functional medical doctors, naturopaths, and others became my sources of valuable information.

The more I delved into what it truly means to be healthy, the more righteous anger grew within me. I would swing on the pendulum in wonderment from "Oh my goodness, women need to know this!" to an infuriated "Why are we not taught this?" I had been given no hope for getting well simply because there appeared to be "nothing wrong" on the surface. So, for a while, I had stopped searching for answers. But that day in the doctor's office changed everything.

"You will need to take these for the rest of your life," the doctor told me.

Hold up. See, I am the granddaughter of Ernest Toby Vine, a veteran of both World Wars. He spent his 94 years on this earth, very imperfect but doing what he saw needed to be done. So, don't be telling me that there's no hope for doing something about this dark cloud over my head.

I am the sort of person who asks "Why?" probably more than the average bear, so for me, it became crucial to examine the reasons why I had allowed such a holistic imbalance to occur. Every system in my body was labouring, and mentally and emotionally, nothing was functioning as it should. Spiritually, I was vulnerable to legalism, victim-mindset, and religious dogma. There were some genetic predispositions for hormonal imbalance and digestive problems in our family, but research now indicates that genetics account for less than 10% of chronic diseases. That means over 90% of chronic illnesses stem from diet and lifestyle factors. Once I pieced together this puzzle, my health journey accelerated with leaps and bounds.

One morning a few years later, as I sat on our veranda basking in the early morning sunlight, I realized I was genuinely happy. The corners of my mouth had turned up involuntarily, without any conscious decision to smile. It kind of shocked me. Some weeks later a sense of peace followed, and after that, the feeling of being loved without judgment washed over me. All these positive emotions had been elusive to me during my state of profound unwellness. Focusing on them hadn't helped, but when I began to heal my body gently, my emotions followed suit. I had finally come alive!

In the subsequent years, I have discovered that I can also throw myself right back to a state of imbalance by revisiting those old, unhealthy habits for just a few months. But even when, for whatever reason, I have made poor choices and started to slide into depression again, or gained weight again, or found my brain foggy and sluggish – all simply symptoms of imbalance – it is no longer a hopeless or fearful experience, but one that motivates me to get back to what I know creates health. I've learned that being healthy is a sliding scale, and by our daily habits, we constantly move along its continuum.

Through my coaching practice, I have witnessed some beautiful transformations in the lives of those I've worked with. From helping individuals overcome physical ailments and regain their vitality to guiding others in finding clarity, purpose, and self-mastery, I have had the privilege of witnessing many clients turn their lives around.

One client, who was initially burdened by exhaustion, digestive issues, hormonal imbalances, and more, embarked on a journey of nourishment, self-care, and positive lifestyle changes. With a focus on whole, real foods, setting boundaries, and incorporating relaxation techniques and exercise, she slowly improved, one step at a time. Together, we celebrated her vibrant health and newfound energy, as an integrative doctor affirmed the effectiveness of our holistic approach.

In another instance, I supported a client facing surgery and overwhelming anxiety. Through a program that emphasized energy-giving exercises, nourishing foods, and stress management techniques, we empowered her body's natural healing processes. When she received positive feedback from her surgeon about her rapid healing, it was a moment of celebration—a testament to the power of supporting the human body's innate capacity to heal.

There are also those clients who have mastered their physical health but require guidance for balance in their heart and soul. One such client wrote this review after working with me over a few months:

"Rene walked me through a process of discovering my strengths, abilities and passions. During my sessions with her she helped me pinpoint where I was "stuck" and make decisions based on the testing we did rather than on "feelings". Her guidance changed the trajectory of my life by helping me understand what values I held most deeply and subsequently what career would help me feel most fulfilled. I'm so thankful for her guidance!"

It fills my heart with gratitude to see clients pursue careers that bring them deep fulfillment and embrace their true selves.

The unnecessary suffering I witness around me, observing people trapped by past or present pain and drowning in hopelessness, fuels my motivation. My husband affectionately calls me "The Vigilante," and I can't help but smile. He's not entirely wrong. I do tend to go to "war" when invited to stand alongside struggling clients.

I wish someone had pointed out the light to me during all those years of darkness. But now, being able to shine that light for others gives my own half-dead existence purpose. Today, I am grateful for every single moment of my journey—an affirmation I never thought I would utter.

Whether speaking to a large audience or working one-on-one with clients, I help others see the light even in their darkest times. I am not a healer: I simply have studied what basic things need to be in place for a human body to be healthy. The human body, mind, heart and soul is divinely designed to be resilient and to bring itself back into balance once it has been thrown off. I believe that achieving good health doesn't have to be confusing or overwhelming.

By walking alongside individuals step by step, I have the privilege of witnessing their transformations, as they develop self-mastery, creating a healthier experience of daily life.

Recently, a friend asked me, "What do you do?" Normally, I respond with, "I teach people how to be healthy so that my clients look better, feel better and have great energy." But this time, he urged me to articulate my mission.

"I unconditionally love people and give them hope," I replied. In the end, my journey as a holistic health and life coach has been one of profound personal growth and fulfilment that I will share with whomever has ears to hear. It is not a message everyone can accept – taking responsibility for our own health and that of our families is sometimes a heavy load to bear - but for those who do it is life-changing, just as it was for me.

With gratitude in my heart, I continue to embrace my role as a holistic health and life coach as my life's calling. As women we have things to do, people to serve, lives to touch: Who has time to be anything but full of energy, love and encouragement?

Every moment of my journey, every person I have the privilege of helping, is a testament to the power of the body, mind, heart, and soul's innate healing: Mine and theirs. It's not rocket science: I'm not that smart. But I have seen too many lives improved, and experienced it myself, when simple, natural healthy habits are put into place, intentionally living a life that looks different to the world around us.

When a person heals, it takes time. Cells regenerate, thinking patterns change, hearts become more pliable and resilient. Often it is a slow and subtle improvement that is difficult to measure. It is only in looking back that we can see the path we've taken, the hills we've clawed our way over and the valleys we've trudged through.

So I will continue to walk through the dark with women who are overwhelmed and exhausted - not as a Healer, but as a Light-Bearer - equipping them with the tools they need so they can find the way on their own to good health and balance once again.

About the Author

Rene is a Holistic Health & Life Coach, working with groups and individual women who are chasing the trifecta of dreams – looking healthy, feeling fantastic and having an abundance of energy. Rene has a diverse background in nursing, home education and musical performance. She uses her personal experience in overcoming mental and physical health imbalances to enrich the lives of all women.

Working across Queensland presenting natural health workshops to councils, QRRRN Women's Network, at Seniors Plus conferences and at Australia's Biggest Morning Tea functions, Rene has established herself as a trusted expert in the field. She loves music, candlelight and rainy days shared with friends and family.

Email: rene@seasonswomenshealth.com.au
Website: www.seasonswomenshealth.com.au
Facebook: SHE Thrives Community:
www.facebook.com/groups/shethrivescommunity

Billie Jo Watt

"The wound Is where the light enters". - Rumi

In January, I wrote down that I would love to be a co-author in a book at some point in 2023, collaborating with other women to share our stories and voices, creating a powerful ripple effect of hope, trust, courage and vulnerability. When the opportunity came up to write a chapter in this book, It was meant to be! It now feels very surreal typing up these words on my laptop!

There are so many things I could have written about, so it was certainly a challenge to choose! I'm almost 36 and my life has not been easy. I had a very difficult childhood, extremely chaotic teenage years and my adult life has been full of loss, major trauma, constant battles with my mental health and I've raised my son on my own since I was 25.

I've decided to share my journey of recovery from being prescribed a very lethal cocktail of prescription drugs for a severe mental breakdown seven years ago, how difficult this has been whilst raising a young child completely on my own, what doors this opened, the things I discovered along the way and how that resulted in me creating my business and my vision moving forwards for my work and inspiring others!

The depths of despair

It was 2019. 'Please! Just stop! Please! I can't take any more pain!!'

These were my thoughts lying in bed one morning. I was pouring with sweat, my body was aching all over, I was shaking, my muscles were twitching, and I was in a massive puddle of tears, experiencing major psychosis and extreme depression and anxiety. I had been put on a lethal cocktail of prescription drugs after being physically assaulted by a woman a few years beforehand. I walked into the surgery on no medication a few months after the assault and left with a prescription for four different medications- anti anxiety tablets, anti-depressants, the highest dosage of Valium and the highest dosage of a sleeping tablet.

Within a few months, instead of being "better", I had put on a stone in weight, I had no energy, my legs felt very heavy, I was breathless when walking, I looked so ill, huge bags appeared under my eyes and if anyone looked me directly in the eyes, I appeared a million miles away. I wasn't present. I was completely detached, floating around in an opioid bubble! I struggled to make eye contact and when I spoke I sounded like I was on heroin! My speech was very slurry and I had become unrecognisable.

While going through this incredibly intense period of my life I was on my own with my son, and to make it even worse he had witnessed me being attacked. It was heartbreaking. Our life changed overnight and it's something no mother and child should ever have to go through.

I was kept on these life debilitating medications for over two years, way longer than I should have been. I was too unwell to question anything. The doctors turned their back on me altogether, with no regular phone calls to ask me how I was getting on or to start a detox plan. I was standing in the kitchen one day whilst my son was at school and as I took them out of the cupboard, suddenly, I had this massive light bulb moment....

it was sitting in the palm of my hand and this voice in my head screamed why are you taking this? You don't need to! I collapsed onto the floor, letting these mega intense emotions come up. The tears would not stop. The combination of meds had stopped me from "feeling" for almost three years. I was always numb and unable to shed a tear for a very long time...but the floodgates opened and here I was, with this huge release and epiphany.

I phoned the doctor and questioned why they had never taken me off them sooner. I could not believe it when the doctor I spoke to admitted she was shocked to read the duration of time I'd been prescribed them all. She apologised on behalf of the surgery and said it was apparent that because I'd been passed from doctor to doctor constantly in that timeframe, everyone that I'd had a conversation with continuously put through a repeat prescription without checking or questioning anything. Even just writing this produces waves of emotion because I lost so much of my life to their lack of professionalism. Time that I can never get back. So much haziness, so many parts of my life that are extremely blurry and of course the upset it brings knowing how much I struggled being a mum back then too and what it must have been like for my son. I had become majorly agoraphobic- I didn't like being outside because I didn't feel safe due to being assaulted. Panic attacks happened daily, for years, trying to leave the house and out in public too. I don't say this lightly- it was a living hell. I lost my drive for life, I was in survival mode, I did what I could every day and sometimes that looked like just barely managing to keep up with the housework and making sure we were fed. I still managed to do fun activities with my son at home, but social interaction was very difficult with anyone else apart from my boy.

I can see now upon reflection, that phone call was the catalyst for the complete transformation that I've had since 2018.... but I can safely say, it has been the most difficult and painful yet equally beautiful thing to go through.

The long road to recovery

I started reducing the dosage of all the meds in December 2018, a year after moving areas and it took a year to completely detox from them all. A whole year of internal chaos and unbelievably loud chatter in my mind and if I'm being honest there was a few times I thought I wouldn't make it to the other side. The physical symptoms were honestly horrific. As the psychological symptoms worsened, I genuinely thought I had lost my mind altogether. I would plummet deeper and deeper into despair, doubting I had the strength to keep going. I remember one day out of curiosity I took the leaflet out of an old box of Valium and read through it, and at the very bottom in tiny black writing it clearly stated no one should be prescribed this for more than four weeks. FOUR WEEKS?!! All of a sudden, a tsunami of anger erupted inside of me, and anger was something that kept arising for a very long time!

Down the rabbit hole of discovery

Here's the part where it gets magical.... As soon as the decision to change for the better was made, the universe did it's incredible thing and supported me in more ways than I could ever have imagined, creating a whole new world! Within weeks, I started to meet the right people at the right time, and I was encouraged to explore the world of self-development. I started meditating, which was very uncomfortable to begin with, but I stayed with it. I was led to breathwork and explored that for a while, then I met someone "by chance" (which I now fully believe there is no such thing!!) and this person introduced me to oracle cards. I'd heard of tarot cards before but never Oracle. The woman gifted me a deck of her old oracle cards to take home and have fun with.

Little did I know at that time just what would end up manifesting as a result of this! It started off as a hobby, I would pull myself a card every day and then practiced giving myself an in depth reading which blew me away, then I practiced reading for friends and family – well, the people in my life that were open minded enough to give it a go! Their feedback was so encouraging, and with that encouragement and lovely reviews and a newfound confidence within myself I ended up taking it online!

Back then I ran a Facebook mental health support group- something I was passionate about because of my own struggles. I decided to push the "go live" button one day despite being so anxious and pulled cards for people who were online at that time. It was such a liberating experience, and I couldn't wait to do it again. I started doing live readings regularly in there and other groups!

Clairvoyance opens up

2019 was a crazy year! I visited a friend at Hogmanay and was still there the next day. It was early afternoon and as I was standing at her back door looking up at the sky, I could not believe my eyes. Tiny sparkles of light, hundreds of them, lit up the entire sky and a few minutes later I saw what I can only describe as a transparent angel floating around coming down onto the grass and back up to the sky again. I couldn't see a face; it was more a see-through shape of an angel with huge wings, and it was made up of sacred geometry shapes! I cried; I'd never witnessed anything like it.

A few months later and another friend whom I hadn't seen in person for around 20 years had reached out and asked if I could pull him a few oracle cards. Later that night when I got the cards out, I sent him a voice message with what came up for him and my voice started to change, it was deeper! I then got lots of images appearing in my mind's eye- I had no idea what was happening but knew I had to pass it on! My friend was gobsmacked and proceeded to tell me this was his uncle who had died only a few months beforehand! This was my very first mediumship experience and I've since went on to pass on hundreds of messages from people's loved ones in spirit, which I'll be writing about in another book one day!

A friend passed away in September 2019 just after I came back from a plant medicine retreat, then the following month an ex-boyfriend took his own life. Two months later my grandfather passed away. I was so consumed by grief and shock-. three bereavements in four months, a friend, an ex-lover and a family member, it was horrific. Looking back, it was so confusing because I was starting to experience mediumship whilst so many people were dying!

In between these bereavements I got attuned to reiki level one. My whole vibration changed, it was so powerful and when I look back now, I realise it helped a lot with grief during that time. I use Reiki in my work now and can send it to anyone, anywhere in the world!

More grief, more trauma

March 2020 arrived and the whole world changed as we knew it. Weeks into lockdown and one of my old good friends committed suicide. I was already majorly struggling with grief; I couldn't take any more. I then had a bad accident! I didn't break my ankle but badly sprained it- I was off my feet for six months then could only walk a very short distance for another year. All while trying to cope with lockdown, being a single parent, in a state of shock still with all the loss and not even realising how much my mental health was rapidly deteriorating due to insomnia because of where I lived. My son grew up too quick, helping me with housework and I spiralled into major depression! We were stuck in the house together most of the time, I had very little support around me.

I decided to start a new FB group for connection during lockdown – and was gobsmacked at what manifested! Almost

1,000 people ended up joining and I ended up organising an online healing festival in there! 30 people from different countries came forward to be a part of it- it was absolutely amazing! I ended up closing it after two years but Our Temple of Light served its purpose and brought so much healing and joy to many hearts across the world!

I discovered sound healing with crystal singing bowls during this time. I couldn't get enough of the frequencies they emit, and I felt like I was healing a lot with them, so much so I ended up buying my own set. When they arrived, I just knew sound healing was meant to be a big part of my journey! I decided to study them so I could then use it for future clients.

We relocated again last year after I had another huge mental breakdown and we had only been moved in ONE WEEK when we had a family bereavement then three friends passed within a two-month period. Yet again I was overcome with so much grief- ironically, while trying to rebuild my life and move on!

While healing from everything that I'd been through in recent years, I finally decided it was time to become self-employed but only working part-time, due to a disability I now have after the accident and because I'm a single parent but I felt that fire roar in my belly and nothing was going to stop me no matter how difficult it was going to be!

Where I'm at now

I launched my business in December! I use the things that have helped me for clients so that they too can alchemise fear into trust and love again. Holistic healing, using oracle/tarot cards, mediumship and focusing on self love/heart healing have all helped me tremendously and I am so full of hope and trust for the future for the first time in my life! I did public readings at local markets twice this year and loved it! Up until now most of my readings have been over video calls or voice recorded then sent to my clients so this was a fantastic experience and I look forward to doing many more!

My abilities have developed so much in the last five years- it started off with just pulling cards and reading from the guidebook and now through opening up my third eye chakra, meditating and studying a lot, I now use clairvoyance, clairsentience, claircognizance and clairaudience and channel information through me to assist my clients with where they are at in life right now and how they can move forward with confidence and clarity! I also run learn to read Oracle card and psychic development workshops!

I started hosting online women's circles in 2021, something I was guided to do after healing my trauma around women after being assaulted! I've been blown away by everyone's courage, love and empathy and hearing what each woman goes through and the trust they put in me as I hold space... Oh my heart! It's been seriously life changing!

You have a voice for a reason!

I've shared my experience with medication to highlight the dangers of being on certain drugs for way longer than you should be and because I'd love to see massive improvements to the healthcare system in Scotland and how they deal with patients in times of crisis. I recommend trying alternative therapies - sound healing and energy healing has helped me immensely hence why I'm now using them as part of my career.

I was completely let down and felt so alone, vulnerable, weak, scared and suicidal and I hate to think of anyone else ever going through what I did. Always speak up and make sure you are getting enough support! There is no shame in being human!

Every single step has gotten me to where I am today- every therapy, every meditation, every course I've studied, the plant medicines I've tried, including Ceremonial Cacao- one of my favourite things in the world now! The people I've met, the vulnerability and courage I've tapped into. It's changed everything!

I want to show other people who have also had extremely tough lives and who may be battling with their mental health, medication, grief or going through abuse that healing IS possible, and not only is it possible but you can go on to create the most beautiful life for yourself, in time, with patience and with so much determination, strength and courage.

I still experience PTSD triggers occasionally, but they've became much less frequent with the inner work I've done and continue to do! Healing is an ongoing journey, and we have to learn collectively how to feel, heal, process and move on from the things that we've experienced and not let our past traumas define who we are in this beautiful present moment and our visions for our futures. Every one of us has something unique to give to the world and it's very sad to think so many people let fear or past trauma hold them back. We each need to do our part to heal ourselves, our families and our future generations...

Every trauma that I've experienced so far in my 35 years of life has constantly shown me that I am stronger than I realise for getting through the darkest of storms and rising up again and again. If I can do it, so can you!

If you'd like to chat with me about anything I've mentioned in my chapter please do reach out, I'd love to hear from you!

This is just the beginning of my career and I'm so excited to see where it takes me- one things for sure- it will be full of magic, mystery and adventure!

Make the impossible possible- I have!

Spread your wings and fly!

"Change the way you look at things and the things you look at change- Wayne Dyer".

Billie x

About the Author

Billie lives in Scotland with her eleven-year-old son Josh. She runs her business, Dancing with the universe, from home, working online and will be bringing her work to the city centre of Aberdeen soon- including sound healing, women's circles and her unique oracle/tarot card/ intuitive guidance readings!

She is qualified in care and travel and tourism and worked in the care field for many years. Billie runs a community on FB called Ripples of Light- she loves encouraging people to shine! She is a natural born leader!

In her spare time, she loves playing the guitar, writing, studying many topics including shamanism, divination and meditation, exploring nature, catching up with friends and going to see music gigs!

Facebook: Dancing with the universe
Instagram: dancingwiththeuniverse22
Website: Dancingwiththeuniverse.co.uk

Donna-Lee Wynen

'The universe rewards action not words' - Insight Seminars

Showing Up

My heart wants to write about the hardship I've faced in my life and how I have established and developed the characteristic traits of being able to rely and depend upon my ability to constantly show up for myself. My focused determination has given me the courage to take risks, learn from mistakes while I participate in life's opportunities and lessons.

I've chosen to find the good in the not so good, otherwise my life would have been too painful to live. I've learnt to bounce back no matter the challenges I've faced. I know I am a beacon of light that is striking, direct and fierce, I am here to activate divine energies that reside within you that will remind & rekindle your soul heart fire. When your faith has diminished, I'm the sunshine that restores hope, that's why I'm here as a voice of impact to share my story with you.

Adversity has given me the experience of exploring my capacity to befriend resilience. I've grown up in unstable and awkward family dynamics. I've learnt self-reliance at a young age, and I've participated in difficult relationships and lived through tragedy. I am not my fears, vulnerabilities, untruths, or insecurities, I am who I am a creative art piece in continuous design who is always enough.

As I reflect, I see fragments of my life coming back to support me where I am now. I know my past doesn't define me; however, it's shaped who I am today. In that reflection, I see the steps of growth from being a maiden, a mother and now a crown, I am living breathing wisdom. I acknowledge, recognise, and value these qualities that I have so long desired. I now hold myself in a loving embrace, as I did my newborn babies. This intrigues me as I witness the impact of falling in love with myself and the follow-on effects that continually benefit my life and personal growth.

> 'Knowing yourself is the beginning of all wisdom' Aristotle

As I pause, breathe, and allow my heart space to have its voice, I feel the sensations of deep heartache, anxious nervousness and the overwhelming warm rise and fall of emotions that triggers my tears to well in my eyes and fall down my cheeks. I sink into my heart's calling, my body slumps, my fingers continue to type through the blur, as the river of tears reveals the truth.

I was slowly dying; I was slipping away from the true essence of my existence. I remember looking closely at my eye's reflection in the mirror, I was overwhelmed with the depth of sadness I witnessed in that moment, I was the abyss. I'd retreated into the sacred recesses of my oblivion, in there no one knew my feelings, thoughts, or my secrets.

I'd been living in a domestic violence relationship for twenty-five years, and I was paralysed by my own fear of the unknown. How was I going to leave my relationship? My excuses were real to me. How was I going to move away while living in a remote outback town and survive on my own with two children? It felt impossible to get away and it was for a long time.

I'd been kidding myself for years, as I brushed aside the obvious signs and feelings, knowing I wasn't happy nor safe. I felt powerless, I doubted myself and I lacked trust in my judgments. I was stuck in the patterns of controlled behaviour, mind games and untruths. I second guessed my gut instincts until I no longer recognised my own voice.

Retreating was my survival place; I'd withdraw, recoil inwardly and become quiet and resentful. My persona would alter, and I'd feel my body and gut become hyper-vigilant. This instantly triggered my anxiety and the sense of prepared trepidation. My body would signal the warning signs 'It's survival mode time, get ready to walk on eggshells and negotiate the land minds!'

It's remarkable what my body became accustomed to, react, protect & manage evasive action plans in situations that were often a false sense of security. Over time this inner discord affected me physically, mentally, emotionally, and energetically. The side effects of fatigue and emotional distress would flatten my energy & willpower. My physical body would get energetically chorded and I would become instantly ill with bronchitis & pneumonia, and I still didn't leave!

The intercom of conversations from my mind would circulate all the thoughts that I would grapple at, about what I could do better to make things easier. It was surely my fault that this was happening. I'd make personal compensations so that I could manage the difficulty of what often occurred in these times. I felt useless and powerless, I second guessed my own instincts and I lacked confidence to speak up for myself. I was living in my own paralyses.

Having an opinion didn't always meet with a compromise. The controlling behaviour progressively got worse over the years, and I relinquished my power to speak up. Conformity was a conditioned behavior that I became accustomed to, it was easier to oblige than react. I wasn't yet brave enough to listen to my heart.

As I look back, I see these patterns have been founded in my childhood. I'm the eldest of five and my father and mother married young due to my birth. Being first born came with instinctual responsibilities, my role as a babysitter of my siblings started in my infancy. I also worked out how to keep myself safe as I could sense when my parent's moods and emotions would change.

I realise now, I've spent most of my life in domestic violence environments and can see how being conditioned and controlled by the incidental actions of another is camouflaged care. The negative bias continually permeates the psyche like a crepitus dark creature.

Over time narcissism, personal reticule, isolation, brainwashing, emotional and verbal abuse, sexual blackmail, coercion, social exclusion, blamed for their behaviour, threats, and intimidation when children became a part of the dynamic; were circumstances that eventually had the sole purpose of wearing me down.

> "You may encounter many defeats, but you must not be defeated. In fact, it may be necessary to encounter the defeats so you can know who you are, what you can rise from, how you can still come out of it." — Maya Angelou

I can totally relate to why women don't leave abusive relationships. It takes courage, bravery, guts, determination, and a tonne of wilful want, to say 'Fuck it I've had enough! What do I have to lose? What's the worst thing that could happen?'

I'd been planning to leave the relationship after my son finished high school, as I didn't want to cause any upheaval in his final year of education. Unfortunately, his sudden death delayed the process of me leaving that year. I remember thinking to myself while I hugged my lifeless boy in my arms, 'How can I leave now? It took me another four years before I finally found the courage to leave and not feel guilty in walking away.

During those years, I felt trapped, my confidence clouded by overwhelming self-doubts and insecurities. I needed help and I secretly sought out professional guidance counselling and had phone consultations with my naturopath. The turning point however was when the local community nurse recommended that I see a psychologist. I was hesitant at first as I thought it meant I was crazy. I found these sessions to be a safe place to escape and realign myself.

I learnt CBT Cognitive Behavioural Therapy which helped me to understand that the manipulative talk and self-conflicting thoughts I'd been conditioned to for decades were not true. I could finally see a way out!

I silently planned my escape. I wanted a better life for my daughter as I could see that I was repeating my childhood learnt behaviour patterns. It also became clear to me that I was role modelling similar behaviour as a parent to my children. I wasn't going to allow this to continue, I'd had enough. If life was going to change then I had to be the change. I focused on my side hustle business Free-Spirit Healing, and I registered my business name, gained an ABN & declared an income to build security for my own future hope. I knew exactly what I was doing, I was building my self-confidence, independence and was practicing changing my thoughts.

I was curious to further expand my knowledge of bodywork. I'd spent twenty years working with clients within my community and saw the benefits both personally and professionally of the potential for natural therapies and what scope of perspective it could offer. Studying became my life raft and sanctuary of peace. I sought out courses that sparked my intrigue, and I wanted to know more about what I was seeing, hearing, and feeling in client sessions as I developed my intuitive body work skills.

It was difficult getting away, the long distances to attend classes, combined with conflicting and interrogative conversations prior to leaving was draining upon my nervous system. Every time I planned to attend a course I was met with resistance, conflict & undermining personal ridicule. The ruminating thoughts were triggered, and I would feel guilty and remorseful. My inability to speak up for myself was frozen solid in my fear of the repercussions that became a consequence of my actions. I was constantly balancing my wellbeing and my deep concerns of how my daughter would cope while I was away. It was exhausting living in constant vigilance.

The mind game phase deliberately deconstructed any strength

of character that I showed. I would literally practice what I'd say over and over before I'd nearly vomit the words out to announce I was going away. It was ridiculous of me to leave it to the last minute. I find it quite incredible that I let this happen, and that I was conscious of the effects it had upon both my daughter's life and mine. I feel there's a false sense of security in domestic violence that kept me paralysed, silenced, and believing that this was love?

I continued to take the risks in studying and managed to manoeuvre around the hardships and relished my time away to recalibrate and take respite. I attended courses in self-development, mental health, completed my Masters in Reiki, Isis Seichim, Karuna Ki energy healing and became a Practitioner in Aura Soma.

In 2010 I had a chance meeting with a body worker who introduced me to Ortho-Bionomy. I'm certain my son had something to do with this connection as I believe Ortho-Bionomy saved my life. This gentle body work resonated with my intuitive vibration and inspired that spark of inquisitive desire to further my body healing knowledge.

I have no idea how I kept going other than I had a goal and I went for it. Ortho-Bionomy gave new direction and a chance to explore freedom and manifest independence. I developed my massage clinic business and I secretly saved money, worked tirelessly, stayed super fit, kept striving and showing up. I made the best of my tenacious ability to face treacherous grounds, cope with inconceivable losses and celebrate the triumphs of my endurance.

In 2014 after twenty-five years in the relationship, I was told to go! The decision was made for me, I'd been given permission to leave! I didn't hesitate, I began gathering my things, knowing all the while the situation could change at any moment. I'd never forgotten the words my ex-partner had spoken to me in all sincerity after our sons' death. 'I could shoot us all and we'd all be together' was a good reason to keep navigating the tough stuff and get out.

> 'The people who are truly strong lift others up. People who are truly powerful brings others together' – Michelle Obama

It's been ten years since I left that relationship and reclaimed my life. Although tough and liberating, I believe being able to cope in those hardships that I've saved my daughter from repetitive patterns of control and given us both the freedom and resilience to lead our own lives.

I love that I am an accumulated collection of my choices and I see my life as my own educational institution, the University of Donna-Lee Wynen. I've passed, failed, made mistakes, celebrated successes while learning to be comfortable in my own skin, that is where my peace resides.

My Vision

*'That every human being can find
self-compassion, kindness, and presence.'*

For the past thirty-five years I have been facilitating holistic wellbeing with clients. I have a wealth of knowledge and accumulated wisdom that is grounded in my heartfelt experiences.

I have witnessed how working with people's body's can improve their energy fields and alter their perspective to see differently. Providing a safe supportive environment, whether it's online or in person is the first step to inviting the space for change. People respond beautifully to kindness when they are seen, heard, reassured, and valued; barriers become breakable, and direction becomes clear.

In life we encounter different scenarios, conditions or circumstances that can affect the body's well-being, physically, emotionally, mentally, and energetically.

These imbalances destabilise our body's frequencies and can cause a sense of misalignment. This can feel like confusion or displacement, loss of direction or at a crossroads. There can be ailments of unexplained body pain, recurring illness, trauma or accidents, loss, loneliness or isolation, tragic life events and unexpected changes that disturb the equilibrium of the body's wellbeing.

Balancing our body benefits all levels of our consciousness. Meeting people on their terms gives the body space to recognise safety and initiate the natural process of self-correction. I have witnessed remarkable shifts in people's consciousness, in relation to holistic body work. For example, a single Mum managing her eight-year-old son who is on the Autism Spectrum with Sensory Processing Disorder & Irlen's Dyslexia, found her sessions to be, I quote 'It is an hour to myself, talking, learning mental work to gain a positive approach, relief from my body tension and taking time to help myself.' Her son is now eighteen years old & nearing completion of year twelve, she's never given up even when she wanted to. She said, 'I used to think I was a bad Mum and now I know I'm a good Mum'. Her sessions have taught her how to notice and trust her instincts.

I believe being able to meet people where they are at is what makes transformational intuitive body work profound. By helping someone to recognise how they can relate to themselves is life changing. I quote an example from a client 'I felt 100 times lighter than when I went in. I felt that a great weight was lifted from my shoulders. The more often we met, the more she gave. She not only eased my physical ailments, but she also brought me back to being the person that I had lost. She brought me back to me.'

I have helped hundreds of women find themselves, through body work, life guidance or energy clearing, I hold space for them to regain their sense of clarity and knowing within.

A client shared this 'I remember the first time I entered the room, and I didn't want to go anywhere near you and you respected that, and let me work through what I had to do before we even started, and that was the beginning of a beautiful relationship.'

My mission

*'To empower people to notice & trust
their own relationship with their body.'*

I empower people to remember that they are the change they dream of and that nothing stands in the way of them taking a chance on themselves. Progress is showing up and doing the action steps which in turn sparks change and reveals the hidden strengths within us. From this I believe we begin to dare to embrace our vulnerable insecure selves and become the growth we all desire.

I see all too often the fast-paced treadmill-like lifestyle that keeps people in a vigilant state of fight, flight, freeze response. Our bodies cannot sustain this pace, and over time the human body will make compensations for its misalignments. It will alter its function to survive and can completely break down if the signs and symptoms are ignored.

The pause gives us time to rest, recover, and nourish sustenance into joy. This is why I want to develop a 'less is more' online program that would help people understand how they can make a difference in their own life. It would be a resource of support that's filled with practical self-care and wellbeing techniques that spark joy, encourage play, and invite us to give self-care wellbeing a go.

I have sixty years of knowledge that I passionately share with my clients and community. My enthusiasm is inspiring and I love seeing others succeed. I currently present to community groups, organisations, education faculties and the public.

My knowledge and practicality of self-care wellbeing is easily translated and taught. People quickly notice the subtle freedom of movement available in their body and want to know more. Self-care wellbeing unravels the mind and gives the breath space for our self-correction to initiate.

In closing – I would not be here on earth without my undeniable faith, belief and positivity that everything does happen for a reason. My experiences haven't defined who I am, they have provided me with the artistic tools to continually be enticed into the design of my life. Opportunities come to those who are willing to discover the abandoned tracks of life, I believe that's where the treasures of our destiny lie and await our discovery.

'Be the change that you wish to see in the world' - Mahatma Gandhi

Love, Light & Sunflowers, Donna-Lee

About the Author

Donna-Lee is the founder of Free-Spirit Healing based in Broken Hill, Australia. She is a transformational intuitive body healer and spiritual mentor. Donna-Lee has thirty-five years of cultivated prowess in her speciality fields of bodywork, energy healing, holistic coaching, and psychic mediumship.

She currently serves on the board of OBA - Ortho-Bionomy Australia, OBA Webinar Program Coordinator and OBA Instructor in training. Donna-Lee also co-hosts the podcast Wholehearted Soul Sister Conversations, Teacher, and Presenter of Self Care-Wellbeing Practices at BHSOTA - Broken Hill School of the Air and Best-Selling co-author 'Voices of Impact 2023.'

Donna-Lee is a fiercely passionate hockey player who adores sunflowers, early morning sunrise walks in the outback and is a loving mother of her children.

Linktr.ee: https://linktr.ee/donnaleewynen
Email: donnaleewynen@gmail.com
Mobile: +61 458447298

www.ingramcontent.com/pod-product-compliance
Lightning Source LLC
Chambersburg PA
CBHW050304010526
44107CB00055B/2096